THE PEOPLE PARISH

THE PEOPLE PARISH

A model of church where people flourish

Gerald J. Kleba

AVE MARIA PRESS
Notre Dame, Indiana

Acknowledgments

While there are numerous people that I could thank for assistance and encouragement with this project, I will be very brief. Thanks to the people of Visitation Parish Family for sharing their lives with me. Thanks to the Moreau Seminary Family and the members of the Center For Social Concerns at the University of Notre Dame for listening while I talked out parts of this book. Thanks to Dora Francis Taylor and Rosalie Manz who typed this manuscript and Phil Manz, who made helpful corrections and suggestions along the way. I am deeply grateful.

Any profits from this book will be donated to projects funded by the Campaign for Human Development in St. Louis, and St. Francis Parish in Silver City, New Mexico, as they help to build homes for people who now live in rag houses.

Library of Congress Catalog Card Number: 86-82035

International Standard Book Number: 0-87793-346-4

Book design: Elizabeth J. French

Printed and bound in the United States of America

In gratitude to the Rev. John Reedy, C.S.C.,
who encouraged me to write even while
on his deathbed.

Contents

Prologue

> In 1720 Phillip Francois Renault, of the Company of the West, brought 500 Guinea black slaves to work in the mines of the upper Louisiana Territory, of what is now Missouri and Illinois. This was the beginning of slavery in the Archdiocese of St. Louis. Most of the French and Spanish slave owners were Catholic, therefore their slaves were also Catholic.
>
> —Ivan C. James, Jr.
> *Black Catholics in St. Louis*

It would be impossible to write about the Visitation Parish Family without giving recognition to the fidelity and commitment of people whose efforts preceded my arrival at Visitation: the Sisters of St. Joseph of Carondelet who opened the first black school in 1846; the black community of religious women, the Oblate Sisters of Providence, who arrived in St. Louis from Baltimore in 1880 to teach children and open an orphanage; and Jesuit William Markoe, pastor of one of the two black parishes in St. Louis in the 1920s and 1930s, who was instrumental in the integration of St. Louis University.

Finally, I must mention a few people to whom I am personally indebted: Father John H. Smith and Monsignor Patrick J. Molloy, my predecessors, who integrated the Visitation Parish School in 1946; Monsignor John Shocklee, the Director of the Human Rights Office, who continues to be a great inspiration and personal mentor; and Mother Flora and all the members of the Society of the Helpers of the Holy Souls whose Christlike presence in the black community of St. Louis continues with little fanfare to this day.

Introduction

My first Monday at Visitation I came down to dinner at 5:30 p.m. After the pastor led prayers, he casually asked, "Did anyone come to 5 o'clock Mass this evening?"

Somewhat embarrassed, I replied in exasperation: "I just got here. I didn't even open church. I didn't know that there *was* a 5 o'clock Mass." I found my voice building to a crescendo in a half-irate and half-apologetic fashion.

He took a forkful of salad and chewed thoughtfully before he replied: "Oh, you don't need to open church. We just have Mass in the living room. I guess nobody came." He took another forkful of salad and the conversation ended.

I could not believe it. Dozens of people attended daily Mass in my former assignment in rural Ste. Genevieve. No one came in the inner city at Visitation. And it didn't seem to make any difference, at least not to the pastor. I had better face the facts. I was in missionary country. I was a priest in a parish that bordered on the St. Louis Cathedral, but I was in missionary country.

One afternoon four months later I returned home to find my pastor packing his belongings. He had decided to leave Visitation and to leave the priesthood. I had barely settled into this new parish, and now I was alone and deeply grieved. Two days later I sat in the office of Auxiliary Bishop Joseph MacNicholas and reported the fact that my pastor had just left the priesthood. After some discussion about his problems, the conversation took an abrupt change of direction. I was surprised by the bishop's forthright statement: "Even though you are only 31, I can make you pastor there. There is no one standing in line to get that place."

While that was limited affirmation at best, I accepted the position with a bit of cockiness, aware that I was becoming the youngest pastor in the Archdiocese of St. Louis. Beyond the confidence, though, there was a considerable feeling of fear in facing the black community and awareness of my own racism. There was more than a bit of uncertainty about the situations that I would face in trying to pastor a poor parish in a beleaguered area.

The next day I entered the empty church to pray. I was scared and as out of place in the ghetto as salt in a pepper shaker. Beautiful English-gothic Visitation Church was aglow with the yellows, blues and greens of a sun-drenched, stained-glass morning. All was quiet except for the few creaks that are always heard in buildings that are three score and ten. I knelt in the front pew and clutched my heavy Jerusalem Bible. The joy of yesterday's family celebration for my promotion to pastor had been replaced with anxieties and worries. I tried to pray, but I was plagued with distractions.

How would I do all the work? Would the sisters leave the school and force its closing? Was I safe in this black neighborhood? My mind wandered and I tried to call myself back to prayer, but to no avail. *Where was the checkbook? Were we writing the totals in red ink? Would the organist quit and the choir break up? Would vandals steal the copper gutters off the buildings? Would kids break the stained-glass windows? Was there money in the bank?* Years ago I had decided even distractions were prayers if they were the best I could do. But I was still tempted to go and find the checkbook and uncover the parish financial status. I worried some more. *Would my car be stolen? Was it safe for me to live alone in this three-story house?* I sat there, my head spinning with the pressure and the urgency of the worries. In my imagination I saw myself out in a dizzying Arctic blizzard, unable to get my bearings. I stumbled around shivering and disoriented, yet I could sense a certain Powerful Presence surrounding me.

Finally, a Voice within me spoke firmly, "Sit down and shut up!"

I relaxed, resting my bible in the pew, and the blizzard slowly subsided. Instead of a smooth blanket of snow, the snowflakes accumulated in several straight piles like huge decks of playing cards. I looked closer and found that the white things were really pieces of scrap paper much like those on which I consistently write notes to myself.

The Voice continued, "I'm not telling you that you won't have 5000 problems. I am telling you that you won't have 5000 problems in five minutes! It will take at least five months or five years. That way you will be able to handle them. For you, all of life is going to be like one giant card game. You will have two cards and a problem will be written on each. You will never have more than two problems at once. When you have solved one, you have a discard. Then you pick another problem. Sometimes while you are working on one problem, someone else will solve the other or it will disappear. Again you pick another problem. With you and me working together, we can handle two problems." The Voice was quiet, and I felt a deep silence within.

That inner voice helped me discover the divine center of my life where the reign of God presides. The whispering in the silence and the calming of the raging blizzard was the calming whisper of God's love within. My anxieties were relieved and the heavy burdens lifted.

Sometimes I still fall into the trap of worry and distrust. And then I must withdraw in prayer to that blizzard scene and find peace in the Voice of reassurance and the card game of life. That prayer experience became a pledge of God's friendship. In my pastorate, I resolved, I would be a minister of that friendship, willing to walk with others in their problems. I would feed and strengthen them as a good shepherd. In this way God helped us to handle a plethora of problems that plagued a perishing parish. Through it all we became the People Parish.

1

NOBODY IN LINE

> I have not the shadow of a doubt that any man can achieve what I have if he would make the same effort and cultivate the same hope and faith.
>
> —Gandhi

I knew that I would do something for the parish. I wasn't sure what. I was confident enough to think that I could plant seeds that would make Visitation blossom into the best parish in the world. Little did I realize how I would first have to be transformed by my parish family into a more spontaneous and caring person! That, of course, is the story of God in my life. First, God came to me through a loving family and sound Catholic education. Second, God's call came in my youth. At a time in life when most of my peers were concerned with sports, girls and rock 'n' roll, I was searching for Jesus in daily Mass and religious observances. Finally, the God of the *anawim*, "the poor people of the Lord," was shown to me by the example, love and support of my new parishioners.

Physically, the parish plant I inherited was a sprawling monster. It was a consolidated parish composed both of Visitation Parish, originally an Irish parish, and Holy Ghost, a one-time bastion of German Catholicism. The parish buildings for these two were six blocks apart and totalled two churches, two schools, two rectories and one convent. There were seven buildings, the smallest with 20 rooms, and there were times when I doubted whether I had seven parishioners. This total conglomeration of buildings was referred to by my time simply as Visitation.

However, this is the story of the People Parish, not of parish buildings. The people were faith-filled folks, unlike any I had experienced previously. I guess their uniqueness stemmed from their poverty and their black heritage which tended to be more people-centered with an openness to the extended family. On my first Sunday in the parish, Stella Page hugged me. I'm sure she wanted to allay my fears and counter my aloofness. Mike Moore, a sixth-grader, served Mass on my second Sunday. He led the procession out of church and then said, "Father, you do nice work."

I was impressed immediately with the pride of the parish despite the remembered racism. In the early 1940s there were still rear seats for the "colored." Later, with integration, the blacks were given the south side of the church. When I arrived, 75-year-old Van Perkins always sat tall and proud on the north side because for many years he had not been allowed to sit there. I learned some graduate-course material in human relations from that talkative father of five who was a trash collector. Later I would celebrate Van and Sarah's 65th wedding anniversary with them. That was a lesson in fidelity.

By and large the parish was very people-centered because it was so possession-poor. But one day early in my pastorate our outlook on discipleship and possessions got the acid test. We received a phone call from a lawyer telling us that we had been remembered in a person's will. The total gift to the parish amounted to $16,000. That equalled half of the *annual* Sunday offertory collection. The gift became a challenge to our ability as faithful stewards.

The church says, "Trust in the Lord, share with the needy, and know that God is never outdone in generosity." However, because of some quirk in the mental processes of many religious leaders, this ideal frequently does not apply to religious institutions themselves. These operate on the assumption that once a contribution gets to the church, the call to gospel sharing is not applicable. In making decisions, these institutions or parishes are so confident that they are doing the Lord's work that the call to share their wealth and blessings does not apply. All that brings us once more to consider Visitation's $16,000 inheritance.

As pastor, I have never been able to see how we can ask all people to trust in the Lord yet never invite our parish community to practice that dictum. A week after receiving notice that the money would be paid to the parish, I approached the parish council with the news. $16,000! The amount was staggering. People's eyes bulged! They shouted with joy! Others swallowed hard, almost losing their dentures. Jaws dropped open in astonishment. $16,000!! With the glee of a child in a candy store, they began to enumerate the wants and needs of the Visitation Parish Family.

One said, "The church needs painting."

Another pleaded, "We need a parish van to haul the kids and pick up the senior citizens and shut-ins."

And a third suggested, "Let's get a new stove and refrigerator in the parish hall."

If the imaginary shopping list had been honored, the money could have been spent in a minute. In a loud voice I took over the meeting. It was easy for me to dominate with my six-foot six-inch stature and 230-pound bulk.

"Wait a minute," I pleaded. "We don't even have the money yet, and you already have it all spent. Now I don't doubt that we need things," I said in a more conciliatory fashion, "but I do doubt whether we need all those things right this minute."

I paused and inhaled deeply. I closed my eyes and wondered what I would say next. By this time I had their undivided attention. People's eyes were riveted on me. It had always been easier to talk about ways the church should give its money away when it wasn't my church or when I was an associate pastor with no financial control. I had always talked about these things with a type of telescopic philanthropy, that is, that wealthy churches way out in suburbia or the Vatican across the Atlantic ought to be generous. Now our desperately poor parish had money in the bank, and I yearned for the security it would bring to me as the person who had to pay the bills.

I continued, "I have always thought the command to 'love my neighbor as myself' might be taken literally to mean that if

I spend a dollar on myself, I ought to spend a dollar on my neighbor. Now our parish has more dollars that I thought we would ever have. And I don't think we can afford to spend them in a hasty or selfish fashion. I do believe that all of the things you mentioned are important. However, I doubt if they are as important as the great commandment of love." By now the people were so attentive that no one even blinked. "Visitation didn't have the money last week and we survived. I don't think we ought to spend it too hastily or imagine that it's absolutely essential for our survival this week."

By this time the spell had broken and some of the people got fidgety as they groped to understand what I was saying. Behind their furrowed brows, they were forming the question, Does he mean that our poor parish should give the money away?

Gathering still more courage, I cleared my throat. "Let's say that before we spend any of this inheritance on ourselves, we decide to tithe."

While it was too early for me to articulate it to the people of Visitation, I thought we did poor people in the United States a disservice by allowing them to think they were poor. Poor people have no homes, rags for clothing, no water, no books, no education, no health care and no hope of ever receiving any of life's amenities. No, I would never tell the people from black North St. Louis that they were poor. Only in the upwardly mobile United States would they be considered poor. In comparison with the rest of the world, poor Americans are in an enviable position. Our people were not poor, and they should not be denied the blessing of giving. "It is more blessed to give than to receive." The People Parish must experience the great joy of giving.

Dorothy Clay, a strong, serious woman, interrupted with a question, "Where do you want this money to go?"

"I don't know, and that's not my decision to make," I replied in haste. "You see, I've only been here a little while, and some of you have been here a lifetime. This money isn't my money, and so I can't decide where it is to go. It is the property of the people of this parish. The people should decide what is to be done with it."

The people sat bolt upright with new-found attentiveness. I felt energized and continued with more confidence. "If you are open to it, I suggest that we vote to give 10 percent of our inheritance to the poor. The way we do this is simple. For the next four weeks we print a coupon in the Sunday bulletin. We invite all parishioners to turn in the name and address of their favorite charity. Someone might say, 'The American Cancer Society.' A second might say, 'The NAACP.' And another might say, 'The Shriners' Hospital for Crippled Children.' Now all we do is accept the suggestions. We don't sit in judgment on them. Our premise is, If a parishioner suggested it, that's all that matters. Every suggestion is just as good as the next, because we are all family together. Our job is to give away the money." I could hardly believe that I had said it, but I was happy and relieved. I paused and waited for some response. I asked if there were any questions or comments.

The silence was broken as a mustached man in a three-piece suit stood up. Out of the 30 people gathered, Oscar Washington was the most dapper. I suspected he would be precise and articulate even before he opened his mouth. Weighing every word and even every syllable, he stood for a moment and stroked his chin as his eyes scanned the crowd. In a mellow voice, he said, "Father, I like the idea. The Bible says, 'Those who sow bountifully will reap bountifully.' In another place the Bible says, 'Cast your bread upon the water.' I make a motion that we give away 10 percent of our inheritance in the way you suggested."

The motion was seconded and without any discussion the parish council unanimously passed the motion. It took me a moment to survey the sea of hands and notice the smiling faces before me. Had these people in a poor parish understood that they had just voted to give away $1600 of their $16,000 inheritance? Were they really so willing to hold their possessions in open hands and reach out compassionately to those who had greater needs than their own? I was overjoyed, yet almost disbelieving.

The man who offered the motion, Oscar Washington, noticed my bewilderment and rose again, this time walking closer to the front. "Father," he said, "in this community this is what we mean by *soul.*"

I replied, "Mr. Washington, it's a pleasure for me to be a part of your soul." I warmed up as I felt a smile beam effortlessly over my face and eyes.

Thus, early in my pastorate I was able to share in the soul of the black community. A few years later the parish would articulate a vision for the Visitation Parish Family. At that time the parish would envision the Visitation Parish Family as the heart and center of the community from birth until death. In the years that followed, the parish made great strides in realizing its dream. You want proof? I can't give you any, but I can tell you the story of the People Parish.

When I came to the parish, no other priest wanted it. The bishop said that. When I came to the parish, the people were demoralized and the neighborhood lived under the threatening shadow of the headache ball.

When I left after 10 years, five priests expressed an interest in the pastorate. In only 10 years we had created rumors of excellence and an atmosphere of excitement. Visitation had spawned a credit union worth over $1,000,000. The People Parish had co-created a community organization that reached into five neighboring parishes, had ecumenical support and political clout. It had taken a dilapidated, unused school building and made it into an attractive child development center for 50 preschoolers. Finally, hundreds of new and rehabilitated housing units were in the development stage.

These things are only mentioned to show that something happened. The most important thing is that people came alive and stretched beyond the limits of their own expectations. As a Spirit-filled people they revitalized the larger community with the power of their gifts. That is the story I am happy to share. It is a story that can be duplicated any time the church is willing to risk being the People Parish with a Visitation-type mission. . . . *Visitation Parish Family strives to become the heart and center of the community from birth until death.*

2

VISITATION CHILD DEVELOPMENT CENTER

I do not love him because he is good, but because he is my little child.

—Sir Rabindranath Tagore

Children have more need of models than of critics.

—Joseph Joubert

All who formulated the Visitation vision statement—Visitation Parish Family strives to become the heart and center of the community from birth until death—were impressed, even to the point of being overwhelmed, by the beauty and the feeling of that vision. But we were also taken aback with the demands to understand and incarnate it into the daily life of the parish family. At untold meetings we discussed the deeper meaning of the words we had used in order to frame their practical applications.

Heart—The *heart* is the seat of all emotions. Warmth . . . love . . . compassion . . . appreciation . . . not confrontational . . . My heart goes out to you. . . . The words and ideas came, sometimes very slowly and hesitantly. People feared looking sentimental and gushy.

Center—A *center* is a nucleus or a kernel from which

things burst forth and blossom. It is the hub where things converge . . . a coming together . . . leverage . . . a focal point around which things revolve. Here was a word that called for more thought. It wasn't an emotion-packed word, but more of a geometric point. Thinking of our parish as *center* was using a term that connoted more importance than our people were likely to attribute to themselves. They were not accustomed to the limelight and felt uneasy.

Community—Unity with whom and where? Was *community* just another word for parish or did it designate a larger area? Everybody was in agreement that we must reach beyond ourselves to those in need. No one was interested in either putting a limit on that reach or drawing distinct geographical boundaries. Community is not a crowd; it is a people bonded.

From birth until death—We had to look at *all* the needs of life. We wanted to be more comprehensive than the typical parish which so often focuses only on educating children and worshiping together.

The discussion of our vision statement was frequently vague, nebulous, and left unanswered questions. One thing seemed certain from the beginning. It would not be possible for us to keep meeting and merely talking on the philosophical level. The Visitation members are people with an action orientation. Consequently, from the very beginning our discussion would often focus on an empty school building that stood across the parking lot from the church. The recurring question was, Does our vision demand that we do something with the vacant Visitation School? The building had been closed for years before I came to the parish, and I viewed it as an additional real-estate headache. Our parish elementary school was six blocks away in the building at Holy Ghost.

What were some of the possibilities? A senior citizen center . . . a day-care center . . . a drug rehabilitation program. . . . We couldn't sell the building because it was heated by the parish steam boiler system and so was not energy independent. The more we talked, the more we liked the idea of concentrating our efforts on youngsters.

Anyone who has driven down ghetto streets has noticed

how often youngsters seem to be raising themselves on the street corners. It is a shocking scene. While many have not yet begun school, they have an uncanny quality of street smartness. The needs of these children caught the attention of various members of the committee. They enunciated a recurring theme in the black community, the idea of the extended family and children being the hope of the future.

If we were to be a church with a future, we had to be willing to invest in that future. So, although the majority of our parishioners were elderly themselves, the committee presented a motion to the parish council that we investigate renovating the dilapidated Visitation School as a child development center. The people deliberately chose a name that denoted action, growth and nurturing—*development*. Child care sounded too passive and custodial; we would not create a place merely for snacks and TV reruns.

To help move us toward the realization of our vision, we set a specific goal for ourselves. We would do a feasibility study to determine if the former Visitation School could be reopened as a child development center catering to the needs of parents with 3- and 4-year-old children. Let's pause here and review what we had done.

The writer of Proverbs reminds us that "without a vision, the people perish." We had a shared vision that was owned by the people of Visitation. Visions are only valuable if they move people to set goals. Our goal was the child development center. We were willing to make the significant commitment of a building and untold hours of volunteer labor. We only had a small amount of money, and now that money had to be invested in a professional person who could meld our building, our community needs, the state of preschool education and government license requirements into a viable facility. This was a tall order!

Part of wisdom is knowing your own limitations. But where defeatism merely focuses on limitations, wisdom finds ways to get over, under, around or through the barriers. That is an important rule of thumb in a People Parish. As pastor, I wrote a letter to all the religious communities involved in education in St. Louis and asked if they had someone who would like to work for the summer. The person would have the task of studying the requirements for a licensed day-care center. He or she would also visit other centers and talk with people about the work. The person would also ask the people what they thought about Visitation opening a center. We didn't want to be unnecessary competition to others; our center could not be a success if we forced the closing of another neighboring center that offered a quality program.

The letters brought several responses, but none more enthusiastic than that of Sister Joanne Fischer of the Precious Blood Sisters. Sister Joanne was a former principal who was looking for a new challenge in her life. She came with a gift of organizational skill and determination. She enjoyed boundless energy that was frequently accompanied with a radiant smile. And, best of all, she had an artistic flair and sense of color; she saw the potential in this 60-year-old building. To our delight, Sister Joanne accepted our summer job.

After the long hours and frustrations that the summer held, Sister Joanne finally reported to our task force that the job could be done. All of the day-care sites she had visited were actually encouraging our efforts. Many of them were generous in giving us old furniture, educational toys and other items they no longer needed. Since we needed everything, we never refused a hand-me-down.

At this time an effective parish finance committee was still in the future. It was my job to inform the parish council that the idea seemed marvelous and had my total support — as long as we realized we had no money. Salary for Joanne was all we had to invest in this endeavor. I made the announcement, and the task force looked at me like disappointed children who had been teased with the promise they would go to the ice-cream store when all along the store was closed. The excitement concerning the promising prospects for the building was dashed by the forbidding financial information. I saw the dejection and betrayal in their faces.

In my most upbeat fashion, I tried to respond. "I didn't tell you we couldn't build this child development center. I just told you we didn't have any money to invest in it. We can still do it," I said firmly, half-trying to convince myself.

"What can we do without money?" someone questioned.

"We can begin," I reasoned. "In order to do anything, we need to rid this building of all its poisonous lead-based paint. Now, if we are interested in the project, we can do that. We must ask ourselves this question, 'Are we willing to do the sweaty, thankless task of scraping all the walls and ceilings and burning the paint off the woodwork?' If we are, we are committed to the project. If we are not, then we have just been talking. The parish does have enough money to buy scrapers, wire brushes and fuel for the blowtorches. Are we ready to work?" I challenged hopefully.

I sensed that the people wanted to rise to the challenge but were hesitant. "I know we have limited time and energy to put into the project and even less money. I know we must begin with unlimited faith. We must begin with the type of faith the little boy had who came forward that day when Jesus was planning to feed the 5000. In the face of that hungry crowd, the guileless youngster came forward offering his five loaves and two fish. He did that at the risk of being considered foolish and, more important, with the sad prospect of seeing his lunch disappear altogether. That is the risk we must take. We must offer as much as we have in good faith. Then, and only then, is it right for us to turn to others and ask their support and assistance."

Parish and neighborhood groups and individuals began the dirty and tedious project of scraping lead-base paint. The fact that the project was begun at all was a testimony to the ancient Chinese proverb, A journey of a thousand miles begins with the first step. The fact that so many retired people and senior citizens invested themselves in the work and saw it through to completion was a sign that people were eager to bridge the generation gap. It also pointed out to me that the senior citizen population is an enormous resource. Like all sizable projects, ours depended on a small, faithful group of Trojan workers — Vernon Butler, Tom Dew, Ann and Bernard Cook, John Jenkins and James Herman. Countless others labored in a more sporadic fashion.

The day-to-day progress of the project was not without setbacks. The first of these came when it was discovered there were no blueprints available for the building. The city inspectors would not even consider coming out to see the building unless they first had the plans and drawings that would certify the size of the building, its individual classrooms, dining room and the availability of adequate restroom facilities. We were soon aware that the standards for a state-licensed day-care center in Missouri were much more rigorous than those set for a grade school, high school or college.

It was time to ask for help. In doing so, we discovered that a young parish member, Richard Anderson, was an engineer for a major corporation. He had received his early education in that very building. We called him and told him of our predicament. He volunteered to make drawings of the building, with his brother or his father to hold the measuring tape. The task took up his Saturdays for weeks.

Finally the day arrived when the city health inspector approved two of the classrooms for painting. They had passed a lead inspection. It was time for a party, but it was a bittersweet affair. We needed paint. As chief financial officer, I had to put my Ebenezer Scrooge hat firmly in place. "We can paint these rooms any color that we like, just as long as we remember we don't have any money to buy paint." Once more there was a downtrodden look, but this time it was mitigated by the quiet accomplishment that gave hope.

"Who has all the paint?" I asked in a cocky fashion.

"The paint stores," someone responded. "But how do we get any?"

Then James interjected excitedly, "I wonder what paint stores do with the dented cans of paint. I was painting last week and I sent my boy to the store to get another can of paint, and he brought home a dented can. I used it, but I was tempted to return it."

James finished his comment, and wheels started to spin in the heads of many of the people there. I reminded the people that if store owners contributed the dented cans of paint, they would be able to list that as a charitable contribution and take a tax deduction. Several people made the rounds of paint stores and factories with a great deal of success. It would not be the last time we would remind business people that there was a tax bonus in being generous. More important, they would be remembered in our prayers.

Another hurdle had to be met when the city fire marshal told us the building code required a sprinkler system. In this old building with its hardwood floors and wooden joists, such a system was an extraordinary expense. We had planned to protect the children with simple, inexpensive, battery-powered smoke alarms. The fire marshal would not accept that alternative.

We went to the city to apply for a waiver. After consideration we were told that the type of electronic smoke alarm that automatically calls the fire department would be allowed.

The volunteers continued to work, and everyone considered how we could ever afford the system. Then Sister Joanne recalled a high-school boyfriend, now vice-president of Sach's Electric Company. She invited Al and his family to come to Mass and see our project.

After Mass, the family joined the parish for the usual coffee and donuts, and then Al asked for a tour of the child development center. He was very impressed with the work that had already been completed and commented that some of the newly decorated classrooms were more attractive than the ones where his children attended school in a suburban parish. At the conclusion of the tour he said, "Is there anything that I can do to help?" He listened to the story about the electronic smoke detectors and then responded calmly, "I'll come tomorrow and begin to design the system for you."

Al came on Monday and went to work. At a coffee break, Joanne mentioned our financial situation. Al said he would see that men got over to our place to work after they had finished some jobs in other places in the city. Joanne explained the benefits of the tax deduction for contributed services. That left only one remaining roadblock. Where would we get the money to pay for the system? Once more she mentioned that concern, and Al replied with generosity, "Joanne, I'll draw the plans and send the materials over here for the job. Then I'll send the parish a bill for the materials. My wife and I will send Visitation a donation in the amount of the bill. You can use the money to pay our company. Then I'll send the electricians over to work for you whenever we have the time since I can see that you're in no real hurry. That way you'll have your electronic alarm system."

It all seemed so wonderfully easy, and it was just the price we were able to afford!

In similar fashion we obtained material and labor for drapes, upgraded lighting fixtures, plumbing improvements and plaster wall repairs. The miracle involved in refinishing all the hardwood floors is only understood by those who believe in God's direct intervention. A steam pipe under the floors broke over Christmas vacation leaving the hardwood buckled and dingy. The floors were refinished to a new lustre by the insurance water damage remuneration.

As work progressed, Richard Anderson completed the building plans and specifications. We took them down to the city building commissioner and several weeks later a woman came to make an on-site inspection. She had hardly seen a portion of the building when she stopped and looked at Joanne and said, "Sister, this is going to be the finest child development center in the city of St. Louis."

Flattered but unbelieving Joanne swallowed hard and replied, "We are still a year away from opening. How can you say this is gong to be the finest one in the city of St. Louis? You haven't even seen this place with any children in it yet."

"I know," she said, "and that is just the point. Most of the time people contact us about a basement room or an unused garage, and they want to know what they will have to do to make that into a licensed day-care center. They even ask if they can get a government subsidy. You immediately get the impression they are just going after some extra money." She cleared her throat and glanced around the school gym. "But you people have this big, beautiful building and you have been working for over a year and have hardly said anything to anyone about it. I can tell that any church that works this hard to take care of the building is going to work even harder to take care of the children once they get in here."

There was another aspect of developing the center that progressed about as slowly as the building and with fewer tangible results. That was the formation of the board of directors and the legal work to allow for status as a nonprofit corporation with a 501C3 status. Many of the comments I make at this point also apply to the chapters regarding the Visitation Community Credit Union and the St. Louis Association of Community Organizations.

We must build on the underlying truth that people are faith-filled, competent and want to be in charge of their parish. Frequently in the Catholic church we say this, but then the pastor is very guarded about financial information and never allows anyone to see or sign the checkbook. That type of operation is a denial of all that a People Parish stands for in terms of trust and empowerment.

Almost from the time the idea was conceived, there were doomsayers who reminded us of the many Catholic grade and high schools that had closed in the past decade in the black community of St. Louis. Consequently, they viewed our ideas as misguided fantasy. While that opinion was heard and considered in the decision process, it didn't rule the day. Aware of potential problems, we knew we should proceed in our work as Dr. Albert Schweitzer did in his. He wrote, "Anyone who proposes to do good must not expect people to roll stones out of his way, but must accept his lot calmly, even if they roll more stones upon it."

Since we expected that stones might be rolled upon our path, we thought the best way to insure ownership and control was through incorporation. We contacted a young woman named Anne Marie Clarke. She had been raised in our parish and educated in that very same school building. She was delighted to see the improvements and share the dream. She was an attorney and city judge. Happily, she volunteered her expertise to do the legal work for incorporation. She met with the board to explain the technicalities and to help us write the purposes of the corporation and spell out the bylaws. This was an exciting event because Anne Marie was delighted to share her expertise and the members were so proud of the way one of their own talented youngsters had grown up. In some ways, there was the sense that we were making these efforts for the present generation of youngsters to try to insure their later lives would be as fruitful as Anne Marie's.

When the incorporation papers arrived, signed and sealed by the Secretary of State, we threw another party. It was another important step that made the dream more real. We were finding out the impossible was just something that hadn't been done. People Parishes must always remember that the goal of all we do is to enable people to use their talents and gifts well. Improved buildings are nice and creative projects are worthwhile, but the underlying hope is to help people image the fullness of Christ Jesus.

And so we progressed at a snail's pace toward an opening date in September of 1981. All of the last-minute details were coming together, but because we had always operated on such a hand-to-mouth budget, there was no operating capital to open the center nor any kind of reserve fund to fall back on in case of an unexpected expense.

The board decided to try to enlist the support of some wealthy blacks from the community. One of these was Dr. Benjamin Davis, Sr., a dentist who had practiced in the community for decades and whose children had attended Visitation School. Over the years he had augmented his dental practice income with the ownership of four McDonald's restaurants. The most lucrative of these was modeled like a river packet and docked in the Mississippi River at the foot of the Gateway Arch. While no one on the Board was privy to his financial status, it was generally felt that few black professionals had attained more success than Big Ben.

His son, Dr. Ben Davis, Jr., graciously accepted our invitation to the child development center for lunch with Joanne and several of the board members. He barely got his foot inside the door when his face lit up with amazement. "Why this place is in better shape and prettier than it was when I went to school here 30 years ago," he exclaimed with delight. "Sister," he said with great respect, "I'll tell you the biggest problem you will have in opening this place. It will be deciding who gets accepted and who doesn't. This place is so beautiful that everyone will want to have their children come here."

Ben took the tour and gloated over some of the niceties in the workmanship and the rainbow of colors in such perfect taste. Then he sat down for a simple lunch and listened to our proposal. We told him we needed some operating capital, and we thought his dad might be interested in helping. His face became quite somber and he related softly, "Sister, my dad is dying of cancer and is not able to make business decisions. But I'll be happy to consider how we might help or Dad's name might be used to raise some money." A pall settled on the luncheon.

Some time before we had begun the practice of listing the names of people or groups who contributed significant time or money to the building of our center. We already had two walnut plaques with engraved brass plates handing on the wall. Perhaps we could expand that theme and begin a St. Louis Black Hall of Fame. Dr. Benjamin Davis would be the first recipient of an award and his image and brief biography would be embossed on a brass plaque for all to see. It seemed like a great idea from a motivational perspective. Daily, the children would be exposed to the plaques and a quiet type of "hero worship." The idea was received very warmly by the Davis Family. Unfortunately, some weeks before the award was presented, Dr. Benjamin Davis, Sr., died. His children and his widow were happy to receive the award in his honor and an important tradition had been born for our Center and for black St. Louisans. Successive awards continue to be made each February to mark Black History Month and the Hall of Fame grows larger. Those who are honored at the annual celebration turn in an invitation list. Many of their friends contribute to the scholarship fund and purchase tickets to the event so our original aim of establishing a fund was also reached.

When the bulk of the rehabilitation work was completed in the spring of 1981, Sister Joanne handed in her resignation and told the board she felt the Lord was calling her to a new mission. She had succeeded at Visitation in terms of the building and its fixtures, and she believed there was someone else with the talent and the interest actually to get the program under way.

We were fortunate to find Sister Carol Jean, S.S.N.D., a suburban kindergarten teacher who wanted to experience a greater commitment to the poor. She opened the center with television coverage of the first day. The board, the parents and the staff have developed, and the children are blossoming.

One of the more enjoyable events and a rather lucrative fund-raiser associated with the center is the spring fashion show. Along with the clothing modeled by adults, we feature each of the children modeling his or her best outfit. Whether it's a flouncy Easter dress, a handsome three-piece suit or a sporty jogging outfit, each of the children walks across the stage, turns once or twice and takes a deep bow. It is a delightful way to put the children in the spotlight. The fashion show helps to build their self-esteem and to see that they are worthwhile. In word and deed we are trying to open up a whole new world to each of the youngsters.

Visitation Child Development Center became the parish's first concrete embodiment of the vision statement: Visitation Parish Family strives to become the heart and center of the community from birth until death. It has served its purpose in terms of its educational goals for all involved, and it has been a warm place of the heart for children and parents alike.

Visitation Child Development Center has also become a symbol of hope and pride for the Community. Many important neighborhood functions and community meetings are held in the gym and on the stage of the building. A United States senator, congressman, state officials, the mayor of St. Louis and officers of major banks and corporations have been in the building. They have all been impressed by its fine hardwood gym floor, its blue velvet stage curtain and the beautiful pastel panels that set off the creamy white gym walls. They always comment on the building and, consequently, give their host an opportunity to explain that the transformation of this building was the fruit of the Visitation vision. As they hear the story, any prejudicial stereotypes fall away. They realize they are in the presence of proud and talented people, and they are beginning to treat them with the respect they deserve.

3

BISHOP HEALY SCHOOL

A mind is a terrible thing to waste.
—Slogan of the United Negro College Fund

There is no short cut to achievement. Life requires thorough preparation—veneer isn't worth anything.
—George Washington Carver

No history of the Catholic church in the United States can fail to recognize the contributions of the Catholic school system. The first American saint, Elizabeth Ann Seton, founded a religious order that made herculean efforts in the cause of Catholic schools. The First Plenary Council of Baltimore (1829) declared, "We judge it absolutely necessary that schools should be established, in which the young may be taught the principles of faith and morality, while being instructed in letters." At the Third Plenary Council in 1884 the topic was addressed again and the mandate that emerged was, "establishing a parochial school in every parish." While that goal was never realized, the foundation of Catholic schools did become commonplace in St. Louis. Those schools not only kept the faith alive when the public schools were quite anti-Catholic, but they also helped poor immigrants establish a level of education for their children that far surpassed their most optimistic expectations.

This historical background is important to remind us that the vision of the Catholic church from its earliest days in the United States placed high value on a Catholic school education. Consequently, the struggle for Catholic education at Visitation was in the best church tradition and in line with a deeply rooted national concern. Early in my pastorate at Visitation, we were faced with the closing of our Catholic school. In meeting that challenge, we tried to keep our parish vision statement in mind: Visitation Parish Family strives to be the heart and center of the community from birth until death.

Deliberations about the school began almost immediately after my arrival. With archdiocesan support the parish ran a small parochial school of 150 students in the old Holy Ghost school building about six blocks away. Many of the students were not Catholic, and so the endeavor could be perceived as a significant evangelization effort. Since the annual school budget represented over two-thirds of the parish expenditures, it was a heavy burden warranting close examination. Fortunately, the chairman of the parish council was one of our better educated men, Alpha Calhoun. He was a Catholic high school science teacher and the type of person whose enthusiasm spanned nature from the atom to the cosmos. It was with that same eagerness that he responded to my suggestion that we list the pros and cons of Catholic education at Visitation. Everyone on the council who joined in this effort saw it as a first step in long-term planning. We didn't dream it would have immediate repercussions.

When the council study was completed, we saw that the wise decision was to consolidate with a neighboring Catholic school. That would cut per-student costs and enhance the quality of education. It was agreed this would be done at Bishop Healy, a school that already involved the cooperation of two parishes. It was one mile away.

We had five months to carry out the entire school consolidation. That required additional staffing at Bishop Healy, building modifications, moving the furnishings, and the selection and orientation of the new school board members who would represent Visitation Parish Family. It was a tall order.

Frequently, these tasks seemed impossible, but the needs of the children pushed us forward. If the Catholic school has been a blessing to many immigrants in the past, it is at least as important to the black community at this time. The Catholic school is a place where people can succeed and develop an awareness of being first class in a larger society that views them as second class. The Bishop Healy School Board is committed to the building of a faith community where the person is precious.

In *To Teach As Jesus Did*, the Catholic bishops remind us that the most important things in life really can't be taught. The spiritual values have to be caught through loving example. In that vein the Bishop Healy faculty, staff and school board is committed to working to educate Christian families by building a community of faith. Hopefully children and parents alike grow to see their beauty as brothers and sisters made in the image and likeness of God. To reach that goal several things are required at Bishop Healy that are not usually priorities at Catholic schools.

At Bishop Healy more support is given the parents and more demanded of them. Among these requirements are the spring and fall parent discussion groups. These four meetings twice a year bring the parents together in small discussion groups to learn some aspects of the Catholic faith or to improve parenting skills. Parents also are required to attend the Parent Involvement Program held on Sunday afternoons five times a year. This program focuses on various aspects of education and attempts to build supportive relationships among the parents, faculty and school staff. It goes without saying that the school requires tuition and fund-raising efforts. None of these matters is treated lightly. In fact, attendance at the meetings is carefully monitored by the coordinator of the parent programs. Bishop Healy School believed from the beginning the church teaching that "parents are the first and best educators of their children." It is the intention of the school to support and encourage parents in that grave responsibility. At the time of enrollment in the spring, each parent is reminded that this school exists because of the sacrifices of the many people who work with their children daily. Other people who never see their children also sacrifice; for example, a large part of the annual budget is provided by the archdiocese. Parents are told, "If these people love your children so much, then we are not embarrassed to ask for a parental commitment of sacrifice and love." This thinking works, because over 75 percent of the parents participate in these programs.

Another aspect of the Bishop Healy uniqueness is contract learning. In 1979 the principal reported a very disturbing finding to the school board. Standardized tests revealed that successful and high-achieving students were beginning to falter when they reached the junior high school level. In an effort to reverse that trend, the decision was made to introduce contract learning in the sixth, seventh and eighth grades.

In each subject the individual student and his or her teacher decides on a project the student will do in the coming quarter. A contract clearly stipulating that work is drawn up and signed by the teacher, the student and the parents. If the work is completed, the student is welcome to go on the quarterly field trip. If the student isn't progressing properly, he or she must stay at school and work on the assignment instead of going on the field trip. In any event, the work must be completed for the student to be promoted.

This approach to education demands more work on the part of everyone in the Bishop Healy community. However, the student learns that a person must fulfill the terms of his or her contract. When a student completes the work on schedule, he or she earns a reward. When a student fails to meet the contract, the work is still required but the reward is absent.

The first year the program was instituted it faced the acid test. Some eighth-grade children of school board members were ignoring their contracts. At the May school board meeting their parents joined the other members in voting to deny them attendance at a year-end party. Further, they would have to complete their work during the summer, and only then would they receive a recommendation to high school. The parents and teachers agreed that it was more acceptable for a student to suffer the consequences of failure at 13 than to learn to expect rewards even when failing to do the required work.

At this same time, when Bishop Healy School was improving and successfully serving the larger North St. Louis black community, the public schools in St. Louis were adjudged so poor that they lost their Triple-A rating from the Missouri State Education Department. Inner-city education continued to suffer in all the ways people had come to expect. By comparison, Bishop Healy School was infusing students with an internal vitality of the mind and will. Youngsters were learning how to think in an environment that included love and that hailed each student as a child of God. Some children lived in dilapidated housing, and others missed meals and ate inadequate diets. Play areas were often places where fear lurked. Despite these handicaps the students were given the hope, courage and healthy anger that would allow them to rise above difficulties and aspire to greatness. A mind *is* a terrible thing to waste. So is a body and a spirit.

4

SOCIAL SERVICES

Assistance to the unfortunate honors when it treats the poor man with respect, not only as an equal, but as a superior—since he is suffering what perhaps we are incapable of suffering.

—Frederic Ozanam
Co-founder of the St. Vincent
dePaul Society

At the Last Judgment God is going to announce what everyone had in savings accounts and safe deposit boxes. And then we'll know that there really was plenty for everybody, but people were just too stingy to share.

—Creed Scull
Visitation Maintenance Man

The St. Louis I found in 1973 was a contradiction. On the edge of Visitation Parish in the Central West End were private streets boasting homes that revealed the quiet elegance of the "beautiful people." Splendid century-old stone, wrought iron and brick structures with manicured lawns and formal gardens had an old-world flavor. The Rolls-Royce dealer in the neighborhood looked down his nose at the people who came in to shop for a Jaguar.

A short walk north in Visitation Parish revealed hundreds

of homes that suffered from delayed maintenance. Paint peeled from the ornate cornices and trim, and seams of concrete protruded from the aging mortar joints. There were a hundred vacant houses in various stages of decay. Some were partially burned, others were vandalized of woodwork and copper downspouts. Many had broken windows with tattered drapes blowing in the breeze from the yawning second-floor openings. Between these two extremes were homes where people struggled to survive without heat, electricity or running water. The unoccupied carriage houses behind the Central West End mansions looked like castles in comparison with the overcrowded homes in the parish.

It seems to me that life for the poor is like a human pinball game. They have very little opportunity of being in control. Sometimes they settle in comfort for a while. Like the shiny silver ball on the downhill table, they may find a niche. Then in a moment, at the blink of an eye, everything changes. With family illness, death or unemployment, they are catapulted out of their security, thrown into the rubberized side rail, pushed with the flippers, ricocheted off the electric bells, thrown into the ejection hole and finally sucked into the used-ball reservoir never to be seen again.

Life for the poor is very precarious. Often things just get worse and worse. This isn't a universal statement; there are inspiring success stories that can be told. However, for everyone who beats the cycle of poverty, there are thousands of others who don't. One of those others was Robert.

Robert rang my doorbell and pleaded, "Father, I need you to help me." I ushered him into the parlor and sat him at the old oak table. The stories of human suffering and hopelessness — and the stories of love — that century-old table had heard could fill books. Robert sat his lanky body on one of the captain's chairs and began in a whiny, soft voice, "Father, I need a job and some money."

In the course of the conversation I discovered that Robert was 17 years old. He was mentally retarded and reminded me of the average eighth-grader in size and build. He and two others attempted to rob a barbecue stand. He had a gun, and the owner of the restaurant struggled with him for it. The pistol discharged in Robert's face. The bullet entered between the bridge of his nose and the inside corner of his eye, and left through the opening where the rear of the jawbone meets the neck muscles and vertical tendons directly under the ear. That Robert's vision, speech and hearing remained was a miracle. He was now awaiting trial for attempted armed robbery; the other two men had escaped during the struggle over the gun.

That meeting with Robert was the first of many. There were two trips to see his public defender, three trips to court and several visits to the workhouse. There were some movies, rides to the country, and fast-food lunches in between.

I distinctly remember the first time I went to court with Robert. In St. Louis at the Criminal Courts hundreds of people are arraigned on Monday morning. There are only a couple of dozen courtrooms in the city, so very few of the cases can begin immediately.

Knowing that, I took a book along. The congestion in the room forced me to stand in the rear pressed against a steam radiator. I was wearing my black suit and woolen topcoat. Other bodies, bundled against the ravages of winter, pressed against mine while I enjoyed the advantage of being tall and breathing over the crowd.

Given the press of bodies I was hardly able to open my book, but with some contortions I finally succeeded. It was 1976, the nation's bicentennial year, and I was reading the book from the United States Catholic Conference entitled *Liberty and Justice for All.*

As I struggled to concentrate I continued to listen with one ear as the list of cases was being called. The list seemed endless. Finally the monotony of the name calling was interrupted by a gruff shout, "No reading in the courtroom!" Confident that I was hidden, I looked up peekaboo fashion over the top of my book to discover the culprit.

The deputy caught my eye and his sneering face softened as he saw my Roman collar. In a mild, modulated, semi-apologetic way he said, "Father, it's not proper to read in the courtroom." With red-faced embarrassment on the outside and anger within, I tucked the book under my arm. Everyone looked over the crowd to spot the loathsome critter who was being disorderly in court. Many choked back laughter as they realized a priest was the guilty party. The whispering and calling of cases continued with agonizing slowness and my embarrassment added 10 degrees to my body temperature in the steam bath by the radiator. As humiliated as I felt, I knew my experience was mild in comparison to the treatment I would have received if I had been a black youth reading a comic book.

Robert's name was never called that Monday. His appointment with destiny came later, and it was followed by a five-year prison term.

Robert is out of prison now and continues to spend his days on the streets with little hope and less direction. He still comes frequently to Visitation for help and friendship, and the job or attention that isn't out there anyplace else.

Betty is another person who frequently finds her way to the church for help. Betty is about 40 and a college graduate. She has been in and out of mental institutions, and her condition varies from bright and articulate to total fantasyland. She is one of the many who have been released from mental hospitals in view of the breakthroughs in drug treatment. But she needs a supervised living situation so she will continue to take her medicine on a regular basis.

Betty's family doesn't provide any regular care for her. Fortunately she is welcome to stay with another woman in the neighborhood who opens her home and her heart to her. Betty comes and goes as she will and where she will. Sometimes she has adequate funds, but other times she is broke. Betty is certainly no threat to anyone. Mostly she suffers from her own sense of uselessness. Her talents are seldom tapped except for a few rare occasions when she has assisted in some way at the Visitation Child Development Center.

Freud said, "We shall probably discover that the poor are even less ready to part with their neuroses than the rich, because the hard life that awaits them when they recover has no attraction, and illness in them gives them more claim to the help of others." Considering the lack of sheltered workshops and supervised housing, I'm sure Freud was thinking of Betty.

Dave lives across from church and visits often. After a back injury over 15 years ago, he was declared permanently and totally disabled by the Social Security Administration. Recently, at 50 years of age, he was told he had to be re-examined to verify his condition. The doctor now tells him he is well and ought to go out and get a job. Dave is a victim of pinball poverty. His chances of finding a job are slim. He also feels guilty about the implication that he has taken undeserved money for 15 years.

There are other individuals with other stories. An area of great concern is the growing number of homeless who make a permanent underclass in American Society. And there are the victims of crime. And . . . the list of those in need grows and grows. The situation of being called to help when resources are already overtaxed is a real problem in any inner-city parish. Frederic Ozanam, co-founder of the St. Vincent de Paul Society, no doubt was thinking of this problem when he said, "Charity must never look behind. It must always look ahead, because the number of its past gifts is infinitely small, whereas the present and future miseries it must alleviate are incommensurable."

The doorbell rings and it is time to listen to the story of an elderly person whose minimum social security money has run out five days too soon. Medical costs are rising and fuel bills to heat old homes are skyrocketing. More and more, our society gives old people the gift of life without dignity. The doorbell rings. The phone rings.

Between bells, my conscience pulls and tugs in ways that are hard to reconcile. Did I give enough? Did I give too much? Is the person truly needy? Is the person a con artist? Will the couple really feed their baby? Will he use the money to buy booze? Underlying these questions are some more fundamental questions. Do I trust poor people? Do I have a double standard of honesty? Do I challenge them to help themselves? Do I pray with them?

Fortunately for me as pastor and for Visitation Parish, Frederic Ozanam was born 160 years before I arrived at the parish. Here was a man who was the quintessential lay Catholic of the Vatican II variety 150 years before his time. Ozanam was a French Catholic in a time when the church was little respected and living the faith very unpopular. Under this pressure, Ozanam organized a group of serious students at the University of Paris to support each other in the faith and discuss it more deeply.

The eight young men realized the church had to be reawakened through a life of commitment to the poor; that is the road to credibility. In order to do this, they made contact with a sister who told them of people with special needs. In May 1833, they began their work of serving God in the person of the poor by visiting them in their homes. The Letter of James reminded them that "Faith without good works is meaningless." With this approach Ozanam and his seven confreres saw the possibility of sharing their faith, not just their material aid. By 1983 the St. Vincent de Paul Society, which started so humbly, had 750,000 members in 107 countries on the five continents.

The St. Vincent de Paul Society is indispensable to the Visitation Parish Family. Every Saturday people of the parish go to the bakery of Schnuck's Store to get leftover bread and baked goods. Beginning at noon, people line up to await the arrival of the bread truck. Frequently, this is the bread of life for 50 families.

Another important part of the St. Vincent de Paul ministry is the Visitation Resale Shop. The shop recycles used clothing and household items. For one dollar a bag people select what they need. Some of the regulars are able to get a 9' x 12' rug into a shopping bag and still have room to stash a pop-up toaster in the corner of the sack!

The resale project also involves a wonderful example of cooperation. When I realized that the stocking of shelves and the sorting of clothing was more than the women of the parish could accomplish, I wrote a letter to the *St. Louis Review.* I explained that receiving the clothing could be more work than gathering it. Frequently it arrived with all styles, sizes and weights packed together. A man's woolen topcoat might be in the same box with infants' wear and a girl's sundress. Sometimes people even tossed in torn or dirty clothing and rags. Sorting, sizing and displaying suitable clothing and storing the clothes that are out of season is no simple matter. I suggested that the same people who collected the clothing might have the time and energy to help with its distribution and sale.

The day the letter was printed, Arlene Disch called from affluent Ste. Genevieve du Bois Parish. She said she would be happy to come with some friends and help with the task described in the letter. The day they arrived, they parked their car and approached the front entrance of the rectory. They obviously noticed the bars on the windows and after introducing themselves asked, "Is it safe to leave our car parked there in the street?"

As I invited them into the dining room, one woman explained, "My husband is not happy about my coming to this neighborhood." I told them something about the vision that we were trying to embody in a People Parish while we had coffee and got to know each other.

Several of these women have been faithful to the work for over six years, have made friends in the parish, have overcome many of their fears, and have been generous in helping with other community needs. Several times their entire families have come to Visitation for parish celebrations. Used clothing was the catalyst that brought people together and made friends out of strangers.

Another important Vincent de Paul tradition is the holiday dinner for the community on Christmas. While the delicious meal and the holiday atmosphere are appreciated by all of those who attend, this tradition also has a surprising value for the parish community. We were surprised to find out how many of the parish family members don't celebrate Christmas on December 25 because of some scheduling conflict in their family. In light of this, a large number of people are eager to help in some way such as cooking or delivering meals to shut-ins. They enjoy the festivities when they might otherwise have remained home feeling lonely.

Social service is a vital component in the life of a church that strives to be the embodiment of the gospel. The early church was very conscious of its need to respond to the poor and discover the risen Lord in those who are down and out. The early church appointed deacons to wait on tables and care for widows. That attitude of service is still a requirement in today's church. The danger is for a church to excuse itself from this vital ministry because it is unable to do everything and so the temptation is to do nothing. The church needs to remind itself that we cannot die on every cross.

In my early days at Visitation the constant doorbells and phone calls from needy people were overwhelming. Fortunately, I was able to enlist the services of a modern-day Ozanam, Stacy Murray, Jr., who took early retirement so he could devote about 40 hours a week to helping the poor.

In a compassionate, brotherly fashion he became available to meet the needy, share some of his own spirit and challenge them to greater personal effort and sacrifice. He was always ready to walk the extra mile. In 1979 Stacy received the Community Service Award at a banquet at the Cervantes Convention Center in St. Louis. After the dinner he was honored and received a standing ovation from 500 admirers. The people took their seats, Stacy adjusted the microphone, flashed a boyish smile and pushed back his thinning gray hair. "I want to thank you for the award," he began, "and remind you that my generosity is only exceeded by my good looks." The startled crowd, expecting evangelistic fervor, roared uncontrollably in surprise. He continued more somberly, "Jesus said, 'the poor you will always have with you and you can help them when you will.' If you got some extra time and want to help them, just give me a call. I'll put you to work."

Those who care for the needy live daily the idea of Christianity expressed by Soren Kierkegaard in *For Self-Examination:*

> In our age they talk about the importance of presenting Christianity simply; not elaborately and grandiloquently. And about this subject . . . they write books; it becomes a science, perhaps one may even make a living off it and become a professor. But they forget or ignore the fact that the truly simple way of presenting Christianity is—to do it.

5

NEIGHBORS BUILDING NEIGHBORHOODS

Lord, I pray: Help me to know that our limited charity is not enough. Lord, help me to know that our soup kitchens and secondhand clothes are not enough. Lord, help me to know that it is not enough for the church to be the ambulance service that goes about picking up the broken pieces of humanity for American society. Lord, help us all to know that God's judgment demands justice from us as a rich and powerful nation.

—Msgr. Geno Baroni
Labor Day, 1983

You will want to seek out the structural reasons which foster or cause the different forms of poverty in the world and in your own country, so that you can apply the proper remedies . . . the poor of the U.S. and of the world are your brothers and sisters in Christ.

—Pope John Paul II
Yankee Stadium, 1979

"Father, we got this problem," Claude began. His face contorted in a grimace as he continued. "There is this big old foundation hole behind my house where the Acme Laundry once stood. It's full of trash, weeds and junk cars. The rain stands in the hole and the mosquitoes breed. The winos go down there and go to the bathroom. It's terrible." He held his nose as if to dispel the stench. "I tell you a person can't go out in the yard or sit on the porch in the evening. It's a real terrible problem, Father."

I had barely arrived in the parish and all I knew about Claude Bell was his name and his regularity in ushering the sparsely attended 7 p.m. Mass. My mind and imagination ran wild as I listened to his tirade about the unwholesome surroundings of his neighborhood. It was hardly like any after-Mass conversation that I had ever heard. I looked at Claude with a quizzical frown. My mind reconstructed the scene, especially as a sight to behold from a kitchen window. "Why are you telling me all these things? What am I supposed to do?" I asked the questions with hesitation and anxiety.

"Well, Father," Claude continued hopefully, "I thought that maybe you could call somebody down at City Hall like Father Sal Polizzi does down at St. Ambrose on the Hill. The city would send someone to clean up the Acme Laundry. You must know somebody important too."

The comparison was flattering, but the parallel between Polizzi and Kleba only went as far as names with vowel endings. Polizzi had been born and reared in an Italian neighborhood and had served on "the Hill" for over a decade. It was an Italian area and Italians held respected positions in many areas of St. Louis business and politics. Some of the families were quite wealthy. I was a white priest in a poor black parish in a racist society. I had been a priest for only six and a half years, and I had spent 95 percent of that time in Ste. Genevieve, Missouri. I had no political connections in St. Louis. There was no reason to make a connection between me and Polizzi. However, I was immediately tempted to think about how I might become an influential priest like Sal.

"I want to be a priest who gets things done," I mused. "I want to be a priest who empowers and enables people." Yes, I was sure of that. The idea took shape in my mind. That quick decision in the empty church vestibule on that sunny Sunday had significant impact on my life.

"Claude," I said, stammering, "Claude, I can't be Father Polizzi. I can't call anyone at City hall to accomplish anything."

Claude listened with mixed surprise and disappointment. "Father, I'm sure you know *somebody* downtown. Just think a minute," he assured me.

I could see that this conversation was going to be lengthy so I invited Claude to the dining room for coffee. We locked and bolted the front church doors and headed for the house. In the dining room we relaxed on the high-backed antique chairs.

"Claude, for the sake of argument, let's say you're right and that I do know someone downtown. Let's say I call that person, and the problem of the old Acme Laundry gets solved." Claude's face lit up and he nodded his approval. I continued, "How many more 'Acme Laundries' do you see around this parish? Do we have 10 . . . 50 . . . a hundred? How many do you think? If I stayed here for 10 years I wouldn't get all of the problems solved."

Claude continued to listen with interest, but betrayed a certain fear that in the end I would refuse to do anything at all. I continued, "Let's say I spend 10 years doing nothing else but addressing neighborhood problems and community concerns, and after that I leave Visitation. When I leave, would the only person with clout at City Hall be leaving? In that case all future problems would be ignored just the way the old Acme Laundry site is ignored today. Nothing really changes." Claude's face fell.

I drew a deep breath, pulled my chair closer to Claude, sipped my coffee and resumed, "Let's think about the Acme Laundry site this way. That unsightly old laundry with its many problems is *your* concern. It's outside *your* back window. It is your concern and your neighbors' concern. Now, I'll try to help you solve the problem, but I won't solve it for you. I can't solve it. I won't work for you, but I will work with you."

I paused and was delighted to see a sign of acceptance in Claude's eyes. He hadn't gotten what he had asked for, but he knew he had gotten something valuable. He had gotten the hearing and the challenge that he needed.

The first step was to visit all of the neighbors on the block to see if they were concerned about the old laundry site. Most of them were, but they felt helpless. Next Claude and some of his neighbors went to the Recorder of Deeds Office to see who owned the lot.

The group reported the unsanitary nuisance to the *Call for Action* line of the powerful KMOX radio station. Some neighbors visited with the alderman and brought him to take a close look at the site. Others visited the police captain at the Deer Street Station. There was little method to these procedures, and no one was certain if any one particular activity would make a difference. Finally, city trucks of fill dirt arrived, and a bulldozer graded the vacant lot. This small success brought Claude and his neighbors an improved view from their kitchen windows, and also a dramatic new view of themselves. The terrain was improved, and Claude and his small group of Enright Avenue neighbors knew they needn't sit by idly and watch their neighborhood crumble.

As pastor I had learned some important lessons, too. Listen to people, speak to people, speak up with the people, but don't speak for the people. A seed of hope had been planted within Claude and me that would be nurtured by the close friendship we developed during the shared struggle. We both knew it was there. We didn't speak about it much, because we both feared it might blossom into something bigger and more scary than we were willing to accept into our lives. Nevertheless, it was planted and it grew in silence. We had faced the hurdles that the system always contrives to intimidate or delay little people and make them feel inept. But we had tasted success and now we knew that people didn't have to settle for lives of disappointment and mediocrity. We could strive for beauty, justice and right.

Slowly other needs and concerns were brought to me, to Claude, and to the Parish Council. All of us were open to listening and sharing possible solutions. In doing that, we were becoming a listening post for problems and a place where sparks of hope were kindled. In the old West, issues were frequently weighed, discussed and solved around the cracker barrel at the general store. In our part of the inner city, the hub of activity and haven of hope was frequently centered at Visitation.

Visitation became a pulsating center of activity with the arrival of Cathy Romano. Cathy was a graduate student in the

St. Louis University School of Social Work. She was interested in doing community organizing for her required field practicum, and she came to me to inquire about the prospects.

I told Cathy the story of the Acme Laundry site. I told her about proud people. I reasoned that we ought to build on our past success. Since we had succeeded in the Acme Laundry area, it was likely that we could succeed in a much more attractive area of the parish. Cathy was eager, but hardly knew how to begin. The St. Louis University School of Social Work didn't offer any courses in community organizing. The first step was obvious to me. Cathy ought to meet with Claude Bell.

Claude was delighted and soon everyone in the neighborhood realized that Cathy was the daughter Claude Bell never had. "With an enthusiastic, intelligent woman at the helm, we're gonna get something done," he boasted. The Acme Laundry situation became our model for organizing. We would be very careful not to run over people; we would listen carefully to their concerns.

Claude introduced Cathy to some of his neighbors, and the parish supplied her with the names of parish members who lived in an area called Fountain Park. The Fountain Park Neighborhood was named for the two-block-long elliptical park with a splashing central fountain that graced the area. It was the prestige part of the parish judging by the economic yardstick. It was situated only four blocks from the renewed Acme Laundry site.

Cathy began her visits in a casual, friendly way. Her agenda was threefold: First, she would start to build a level of trust by listening; second, she would help people count their blessings and build community pride; last, she would ask them to list areas of concern.

On the surface, Cathy was an unlikely person to be doing this work. She was the daughter of a well-to-do family from Skokie, Illinois. Her father headed a prestigious Chicago law firm. However, through the love of her family, a lifetime of Catholic education, and a conscious selection of friends in college, Cathy had become profoundly aware of many pressing social issues. She now lived in a lay Christian community and came to the job with a willingness to haggle with Jesus who invited her to, "Go, sell what you have, give it to the poor and come and follow me." Cathy was open to discovering her own poverty and to inviting the poor to help one another.

In a couple of months Cathy met over 100 people. She spent time chatting on porches and in living rooms. As she went, she obtained important information which she recorded on 3″ x 5″ cards. She usually received a warm welcome; people were happy to be heard.

When Cathy had "felt enough pulses" in the area, we decided to call the people to a meeting and share with them their own notions of the best and worst of life in the neighborhood. The list of "bests" was scrap-paper size; the "worsts" would have been crowded on a highway billboard. Home (the fact that it was paid for or that the rent was cheap), neighbors and church were high points for the people; insecurity and neighborhood ugliness were problems. We asked the people if they wanted to do anything to improve the good stuff or eliminate the problems in the area. Cathy explained that she was open to helping them if there was something special they wanted to do. She urged them to be modest in their decision so that the project might actually get accomplished. A complete list of the concerns they had voiced was written on newsprint and hung poster fashion on the wall.

After some hesitation, a rather lively discussion ensued about various concerns. Housing, crime, public drunkenness, sanitation—all got the passing attention of the crowd. Then someone mentioned the need for a stop sign to halt the traffic on Taylor Avenue in front of Visitation Church. Several people got excited about that topic and painted tragic pictures of arthritic people with canes hobbling across the street dodging cars and buses. Soon it appeared the topic of the evening was the need for a stop sign.

I could hardly believe my ears. We had encouraged the people to pick a simple project—but a stop sign? I was tempted to try to sway the discussion to something more dramatic. I had to force myself to remain seated. *A stop sign*!!! I mumbled the words in silent disbelief: "A stop sign? A stop sign?" The decision was unanimous. The group wanted to pursue the installation of a stop sign that could be turned to stop traffic only on Sundays. The rest of the week the traffic would flow at the regular pace. The voice of the people had spoken: *stop sign.*

The road toward getting that stop sign was not smooth and flawless. Phone calls, visits to City Hall, counting the vehicles that passed Taylor and Evans on a given Sunday morning, frustrating conversations and fruitful conversations, questioning city officials and talking to the committee, making friends at City Hall, making enemies at City Hall — all these were part of the process. A stop sign was erected a year later. The stop sign was blessed after Sunday Mass and people were designated to turn it to stop Sunday traffic. The achievement of itself was less significant than the process. People learned that government should and could work. The road was difficult and frustrating, but there was victory in the end.

The Acme Laundry site and the stop sign meant two victories, and the people were batting 1000. A sense of shared commitment was developing among the people of the community. They were honest enough to admit with embarrassment that much of the filth in the alleys and gutters could be prevented by residents who were better housekeepers. Soon a small group of people began to talk about a neighborhood clean-up day. They didn't have to wait for the city to sweep the streets and alleys; people could do that for themselves.

These successes, meager as they were, caught the attention of people in the poorer half of the parish. Several people complained that they were being overlooked in this neighborhood improvement project. In a dual effort to quiet criticism and energize people in another sector of the parish, Cathy began another round of home visits in the Maffitt-Aldine Neighborhood. The same basic procedure was repeated: Cathy started with church members, fanned out to meet their friends and neighbors, and sought to discover their impressions of their community. This area had less substantial housing and more general decay and abandonment than other parts of the parish. It had no attractive green area like Fountain Park.

The neighborhood survey revealed that the community suffered one major blight that the Visitation Parish Family had intentionally tried to overlook; an ugly parcel of land owned by the Archdiocese of St. Louis. There had been a church there, but it had been closed for years. In 1975 the Archdiocese contracted to have the church razed, but the job had been done in a very shabby fashion. The lot was marked with yawning holes, and parts of the foundation and walls protruded from the earth. An enormous steel demolition crane, broken, rusty and partially buried by weeds on the rear of the lot, added to the ugliness. It was the "Acme Laundry" of the Maffitt-Aldine Neighborhood. It was owned by the Catholic church. It was not easy to mouth the immortal words of Pogo, "We have met the enemy, and the enemy is us."

In an effort to make this lemon into lemonade, I asked the people what they would like to see on the church lot. "We need a neighborhood park," was the wholehearted response. I thought that was a good idea. I knew it would be easier to accomplish with the support of the community. Once again, it wasn't easy, but a park was built in about two years. We received help from the archdiocese which donated the property. We received help from the Community Development Agency. We received invaluable professional and technical assistance from a national park design and construction firm, R. W. Booker & Associates. Neighborhood volunteers laid railroad ties to stop erosion, planted trees, shrubs, and laid sod to beautify the area. And when it was all completed, the vest-pocket park was named Blish-Simmons Park for the eldest man and woman on the block. Annie Blish had contributed $100 to the project at the beginning of the endeavor, and Riley Simmons lived next door and watered the grass and kept a round-the-clock vigilant eye. The sore spot became a beauty spot.

During the first year of Cathy's organizing, all of our tangible successes could have been hidden in a flea's ear. The major accomplishment was an attitudinal change and a glimmer of hope in the community. Frequently Cathy wondered whether her commitment was worthwhile. In order to get some inspiration and become better grounded in the theory of community organizing, I called Tom Gaudette, a Chicago consultant who travels the country visiting community groups. He helps inspire and challenge people. His reach is from Oakland to Wilmington and from Detroit to Mobile. At his best moments he is to organizations what Paul was to the struggling Christian communities. At his cantankerous worst he is about as abrasive as improperly held chalk on a blackboard. Cathy needed Tom at his encouraging best. St. Louis needed Tom to remind us that we were not alone and that it takes "a lot of slow to grow."

Tom graciously consented to come to St. Louis and look over our first faltering steps. All he requested was plane fare and a place to stay, and he asked that we arrange for him to meet with people in the community to see what they thought of what had been happening. I told Cathy to invite some of her most enthusiastic supporters to this session so we could determine whether her presence in the parish was worth her salary for another year. The parish had been paying her $400 monthly out of a tight budget.

On the evening of Gaudette's arrival, about 35 people gathered to give their impressions of the work that had been done. I introduced the meeting by describing the church interest in this endeavor as a way to improve the quality of life for everyone, regardless of their religion. My remarks were followed by a salvo of high praise for Cathy's efforts. The meeting continued on that plane until Claude Bell stood up to say his piece. Before he was done, I thought I had just heard a nominating speech for Cathy for president!

Tom Gaudette wrapped the meeting up in low-key fashion. He stood up and looked over the tops of his glasses studying the collection of elderly black people whose every facial line showed hard-won dignity. "Well now, you seem to have something going here," he said with matter-of-fact simplicity. "You want to keep it going. You'll have to keep on seeing what has to be done and getting your neighbors to come out and help." He played with his hands and pounded a fist into his palm. Then he contorted his face in cabbage-patch fashion. But before anyone was too frightened, he flashed a grotesque toothy smile. "You people are on the right track," he assured us. "Now, I can help you if you want me to. I can tell you how other people organized and what kind of work is meeting with success in other cities. People all over the country are starting to realize that things are only going to be better if they make them better." Tom continued now with a fire that didn't reflect in his tone or demeanor, but caught all who were in earshot.

"Today's my first time in St. Louis, and, hell, if you don't think you have problems, then I don't know why you asked me to come here at all. I never saw so many vacant lots. Who owns all that property?" He closed his eyes and held his hand to his head in a migraine look. "And who the hell decides what happens to all the brick buildings that are standing there vandalized in this city? Gee, I never saw so many vacant brick building in my life," he moaned. "So, tell me what you want to do. Let me know if you want me to help. I'm here, and I'll be back if you want me. Let's stop and have some cookies and coffee. Doesn't anybody have beer at this meeting? Hell, no wonder you didn't get more people to the meeting!" Tom sat down.

People rose from their chairs. Some went to the coffee pot while others went to talk with Tom and hear more of his experiences. Some approached me expressing deep concern about the possibility that Cathy's work might be terminated by the parish. I explained to them that the parish council had the final word and would consider the finances.

In twos and threes people began to leave the meeting. One was Mrs. Brown, a determined woman in her 80s who used her cane half for support and half as an aid in conversational gesturing. She was bent but proud, and she reflected a radiance that said, "I'm happy to have survived and still be able to get out and around." I took her arm as she approached the steep basement steps leading to the parking lot.

"What did you think of the meeting?" I asked Mrs. Brown, who wasn't a parishioner.

"I thought it was good, Father. And I'm sure glad you explained about how Cathy was hired by the church. Now I understand how she got here, and I can tell the people on my block that she's not a communist."

Her casual comment shocked me. "Not a communist? I don't think I understand. Why would people say she's a communist?"

"Well, when she has us talk about our problems we usually find that bad city officials are to blame for problems in our community. Then we have to go down to City Hall." We had stopped midway in the stairwell to face each other. "People know that communists are always criticizing our government.

So, they think that anybody who criticizes the government is a communist. Another thing is her looks. People look at Cathy and say, 'Why's a young, white woman like her interested in us and working in our neighborhood?' Then somebody said, 'She's a communist spy trying to overthrow the government.' That's why they think she's a communist."

By this time I was tugging at Mrs. Brown's elbow. "Would you come back downstairs and tell the people what you just said here?"

I realized that climbing the steps for a second time was not her notion of a happy ending for a long day. But she was flattered that I asked her to have the last word at the meeting. When she re-entered the room, I asked the people to give Mrs. Brown a hearing. People gathered around with a healthy respect for the wisdom of the elderly. She repeated her story. As she did so, I could see heads nodding as they recalled hearing similar comments about Cathy's communism.

Thirty minutes later the room was empty and I sat down with Tom and Cathy. "No matter what else happened," I told Cathy, "your first year here is a success because people know now that you're not a communist!"

Cathy's evaluation time was also a time for me to weigh my personal commitment to community work. How could I reconcile community work with the heavy burden of the pastorate? It was the age-old tug between the sacred and the secular in the church. The solution, for me, turned out to be rather simple. I am convinced that once the Son of God became man, then every microparticle of the universe has been touched or has the potential of being touched by the Word-Made-Flesh. As church it is our task to hurry this enormous endeavor of bringing everything into contact with Jesus. When people and human institutions are unjust and do not bear witness to Christ's love, we are to be the transforming element in society. Unless the parish is in touch with the hopes and heartbreaks of daily community life, we really have nothing to offer at the Sunday liturgy.

In my own mind the decision was made. I had no choice but to embrace a pastorate that called the church to deeper involvement. I knew that some parishioners would complain.

However, I had no choice. God's love for me prods me into loving others, especially those who are victims of injustice and on the fringes of society. Despite criticism, I must pursue justice.

This type of ministry would have to be honest, sincere, gutsy and self-authenticating. It would have to be like "gold tested by fire." Without the encouragement of Monsignor John Shocklee and the Archdiocesan Human Rights Office, the task would have been impossible.

Visitation decided to keep the emphasis on community organizing and continue Cathy's job. We continued striving to be the heart and center of the community. However, the newness of it was gone and the honeymoon was over. Minor accomplishments passed as unnoticed as removing one crushed aluminum can from a litter-strewn gutter. We knew that some bolstering was needed. We decided to help Cathy find a support group to share successes and cry about defeats. The sharing would give the participants energy to face a new tomorrow. We also decided to look into the possibility of augmenting her staff by neighborhood volunteers and government-paid VISTA workers.

On the near southside of St. Louis was St. Henry's Parish. It was an old German church that had continued to battle relentless decay. There, too, efforts had been made at community organizing by a group called the Southside Forum. The Southside Forum was more sophisticated in many ways than the Visitation effort. Southside Forum had a streetfront office; Visitation had redone a second-floor rectory bedroom. Southside Forum had some outside ecumenical funding; Visitation had only meager parish resources. Yet the staff at Southside Forum, Sister Jean Abbott, C.S.J., Metrel Scales and Mike Savage, were looking for the same type of support and direction that Cathy desired. They began to meet on Tuesday mornings to review the week and learn from one another. Next, they invited a local consultant, Jim Herning, who had some experience with the Farm Workers in California.

Tuesday after Tuesday the meetings revealed one thing: similar problems. Weeds were a problem on the northside and the southside. The southside housing problem was mirrored on the northside. The northside health concerns were duplicated on the southside. The loitering and unemployment problems knew no boundaries. Consequently, one question arose. Are we going to cooperate and confront growing concerns, or are we going to fight each other over the limited resources available to solve our problems? In the Civil War President Lincoln warned, "A house divided against itself cannot stand." We must stand together. The challenge to unify was before us.

A task force was formed to ponder this idea and hammer out a new corporation. After developing trust and camaraderie, an organization was formed as an umbrella group. The organization chose the name SLACO – the St. Louis Association of Community Organizations. The name denoted openness to groups in the entire area in the hopes of building a city-wide coalition. Prayer guided all the deliberations as the constitution, bylaws and articles of incorporation were penned. SLACO was born.

For many months SLACO appeared to be a paper corporation. Just as a blueprint is not a building, so corporate papers are not a corporation. Funding was proving difficult and without it there could be no capable staff to do the task that SLACO envisioned. We had wonderful experiences with VISTA workers and other volunteers. However, without capable direction, generous volunteers are helpless.

We found some initial success with proposals to religious communities and received some support from several non-Catholic Christian denominations. A year later when the Campaign for Human Development funded us, we were finally on the road. During that first year the Archdiocesan Human Rights Office was often our angel.

SLACO's first priority was to hire a director with experience, competence and integrity. That person had to be dedicated to a Christian notion of community organizing. When we put out feelers for a director, one name frequently surfaced: Sister Mary Dolan. Other names were mentioned in passing, but none with the glowing praise that invariably surrounded Mary's name. She had had years of experience with the Oakland Organizing Project in California and was described as "smart, fiery, dedicated, empathetic and willing to invest her life for the long haul." We called her, invited her to visit St. Louis, prayed with her and hired her almost immediately. Everything that people said about her was an understatement.

The organizational structure of SLACO was now off the drawing boards and beginning to take flesh in real people. The $50,000 Campaign for Human Development grant and the $10,000 grant from the Archdiocesan Human Rights Office formed a solid foundation from which to approach St. Louis businesses. Pointing out the reasonableness of our approach, the documented past successes, and the unrelenting determination of our people were the best method of selling SLACO to others.

In good organizing a reasonable approach must also be tough and determined. An extreme example is the case of a man we shall call Harry Miller—although that is not his name.

Harry was the owner of a dilapidated multifamily building in the parish. The people in the neighborhood had decided that this unsightly, six-family apartment building was a pressing concern as the most obvious neighborhood disaster.

We invited Miller to meet with us, but he refused. Since he was hardheaded and intransigent, we discussed another approach.

A title search at the Recorder of Deeds Office indicated that Mrs. Miller was equally responsible for the building. The Millers lived about 20 miles from their ramshackle apartment building. One Saturday morning around 9:30, several crowded vans wound their way past the private putting green and the pond up the drive to the Miller's mansion. A pixyish, smiling sixth-grader cheerfully answered the door. The group leader asked for Mrs. Miller, and the girl responded, "Would you like to step in? I'll get her."

Thirty people filed into the entrance hall. No one had to step into the living room or the library that flanked either side of the hall. In a few moments Mrs. Miller arrived barefooted and donning a fashionable pink robe. "What are you doing here?" she blustered angrily. "Who let you people in?"

The leader explained that her little girl had invited us in and then praised her on how good her house looked in comparison with the ragtag condition of the six-family apartment building in the city. Mrs. Miller responded, "That place is not my concern. My husband takes care of the rental property." She gestured toward the door, saying, "Get out of here, now, and go talk with him about it."

No one moved. The leader explained that her husband had refused to meet with us. "We thought that since your name is on the title, it would be wise for us to talk with you. You both are legally responsible, you know."

"You wait right here," she said. "My husband will talk to you." With that she left the room. We waited anxiously and shifted our feet back and forth in the deep-pile cream-colored carpet. We could hear her speaking angrily with her husband on the telephone.

Minutes later she reappeared and assured us that her husband would be happy to meet us at his store. Only when she had ushered us past the Cadillac in the driveway did she notice all the yellow ribbons on the trees facing her home. Some of our group had stayed outside to tie giant yellow bows on the trees. The idea was a combination of the song "Tie a Yellow Ribbon 'Round the Old Oak Tree" and the childhood practice of tying a string on the finger to remember something. We wanted the Millers to remember their responsibility in caring for their rental property. "You get out of here," she shouted, "and never come back. We don't need your kind around here." An added sadness is that the Miller family too is black.

The vans proceeded to Miller's store in a sleazy area of St. Louis. The approach to the store was marked by loitering winos in groups of twos and threes; several more were sitting on the stoop. It was Saturday noon and many of the people were in their weekend alcoholic stupor. With canes in one hand and purses in the other, our group of mostly old women struggled up the steps and into the store. Several harassing comments were uttered by the bystanders. Miller was in the back of the store by the cash register.

"You can't loiter and crowd my store. Get off my property!" he demanded. "I'll meet with you outside." We turned to leave and wait for him outside. We could sense the tension and fears of a man who didn't want to meet with us and wanted even less to meet with his enraged wife.

As we waited on the walk and discussed our strategy, our conversation was interrupted by police sirens coming from all four directions. In moments, four cars and seven police officers arrived. There was even one canine patrol. Miller had called them to report that we were disturbing his business.

As we explained our position to the police, one of the octogenarians gently and humorously chided a rookie black policewoman. "This is pretty exciting," she joked. "I'll bet you're plenty scared of us." The slender young woman in the impeccable uniform complete with gun, cuffs and billy club just stared away in sadness.

Even before Miller came out of the store to tell his side of the story, we knew one important thing. Harry Miller certainly got the attention of the police.

"Who are you people anyway?" Miller challenged as he came out of his store. "You're disrupting my business and running my customers away." Then he looked at my white face and my well-pressed black clerical suit. "What are you, some kind of white, liberal son-of-a-bitch from the county? You probably don't even live in the area."

I explained my position and my concern while the elderly people in the group wanted to kill Miller with their canes. They were livid, their motherly protectiveness toward me obvious.

Fortunately our spokeswoman ignored the budding hostility. She calmly began to present the list of code violations on the building in question. She made it clear that unless these violations were corrected and good tenants obtained, we would petition the city to condemn the building and have it demolished.

Miller said, "I'm not signing any list of demands, and I'm not being railroaded."

Since he would not commit himself to any of the needed building improvements, we asked that he at least come to a future neighborhood meeting. He agreed to do this—mostly to get rid of us. The meeting would be the following Tuesday at 7 p.m.

About 50 excited people gathered in the rectory that Tuesday evening. There was a sense of confidence among the crowd as they entered the tidy and organized meeting room. The idea was to exemplify in our setting the quality of care and cleanliness that we expected of Miller's building down the street. The meeting organizers had spotters posted to watch for the approach of the Cadillac. They were to signal ahead so that the gathered neighbors would be on their feet to give Miller a standing ovation the minute he walked through the door. Our reasoning was that Miller would probably park his car in our area with trepidation. He might even be concerned about his physical safety. We wanted to reach him with this gesture of applause; we were sincerely glad he had agreed to come and we wanted him to know that. There is also the gospel notion of loving your enemies to the point of heaping blazing coals upon their heads. Restated in modern terms, it is the poster catchphrase: Love your enemies, it will drive them crazy!

The applause had its effect. After the opening prayer Miller stood. "The first thing I want to do here," he began after nervously clearing his throat, "is to apologize to Father for the unkind name I called him last Saturday morning."

I rose and nodded my acceptance of his apology. Once more applause filled the room. The meeting was begun in a conciliatory and hopeful mood. Before that long meeting ended, Miller had signed a list of required home improvements. He had also agreed to work with us in finding competent contractors, arranging financing, and allowing the organization to screen potential tenants. In principle, all the commitments and concessions that we demanded were agreed upon. The completed work was still a year in the offing, but the first steps had been taken.

Six years have passed since the remodelling of the Miller apartment building. There has seldom been a vacancy in the building. The neighborhood is proud of the new neighbors, and the Millers are getting honest rent on attractive housing.

This case involved going to extremes. This was not the initial plan of the group. All of the preliminary attempts had failed. It was only after moderate efforts had proved fruitless that the group chose to approach Mrs. Miller. Even then, when Miller arrived at the meeting, however grudgingly, he was greeted with sincere and welcoming applause. After all, our efforts entail not merely winning, but reconciling. Good organizing is not turning the tables of oppression and putting the squeeze on others.

With the arrival of Archbishop John L. May, a new era of church was inaugurated in St. Louis. He had a past history of concern for rural poverty with the Catholic Extension Society. He understood ecumenical efforts because he had been a southern bishop in Mobile, Alabama. He worked with a community organization in that city where Gaudette also served as a consultant. When the SLACO Board requested a meeting to thank him for the campaign for Human Development funding, he welcomed us into his office and assumed the posture of a gracious listener. While he found no time to attend any SLACO functions, he used the power of his office in subtle ways to encourage important people to cooperate with SLACO.

By 1980 SLACO was working quite effectively. The genius of the SLACO structure parallelled the relationship between the states and the federal government. Each of the states is autonomous except in areas where the federal government specifically intervenes and in areas that are larger than any individual state can manage. In those instances the federal government reigns supreme. The SLACO structure is similar. Each of the neighborhood groups remains autonomous. Specific plans or problems are addressed and goals set at the regular meeting. Shared information and staff assistance is provided for these individual groups. In addition, each community has representatives on the SLACO Board. Besides overseeing the ongoing funding and operation of SLACO, the SLACO Board decides on priority issues that can best be addressed through the powerful, unified effort of all the neighborhoods.

SLACO has expanded from five to 12 neighborhood organizations. While that growth and success is exciting, SLACO is even more proud that the growing organization has only one additional staff member. That is important because it keeps the budget within reason. Even more significant, however, is that it assures us that real leadership is surfacing from the grass roots. Empowerment and inner direction are occurring on every level within the organization. Hence less direction and nitty-gritty work is required from the paid staff; the neighborhood citizens are able to do much of the legwork.

Though neighborhood people know the process, confrontation is still difficult. After our first encounter with police dogs, it was clear the organization needed to consider aspects of fear and intimidation much more seriously. Extreme power can be loosed on individuals and poor people's organizations who are bucking the system. It is not fair to pretend otherwise or keep people in the dark regarding the possible dire consequences that may be involved with a particular action. At times we had to address the fact that arrests might be in the offing. While this has never happened to SLACO members, it would be misleading to deny it was possible. Each individual must decide what he or she is willing to face at a particular time. As a result of participation with SLACO and media coverage, a leader may experience tension at home, on the job or in the community. SLACO tries to give that person support and encouragement.

Most people rise to the challenge because the organization gives them confidence. They like knowing that they are not alone. Some people become more daring and experience a euphoria from doing the right thing. There is a sense of self-righteousness that they may have seldom experienced before. Many of the SLACO people are older Americans who feel called to live their life to the full. Rather than seeing the "evening of life" as a time for rocking-chair dreaming, it is a time of active accomplishment. They feel the time they have left might well be spent confronting illegitimate authority with a moral protest. They have rejoiced in bringing about changes in law and public policy. Because of SLACO efforts, banks make more loans in our area and real estate speculators face stiffer laws that make their past unconscionable behavior illegal.

All of this implies that SLACO tries to use a balanced and considered approach to community organizing. From board meetings to neighborhood house meetings, two questions always find expression: Is the task doable? Is the fight over something worthwhile? Life is frustrating enough for people. SLACO was not formed to add to the problems, but rather to solve some of them. If the decision is made "to comfort the afflicted by afflicting the comfortable," there needs to be reasonable hope of success. Otherwise, the steps are taken with a sober awareness. As one SLACO cynic said, "Once you offend the rich and powerful, it's not like offending God who forgives. They'll never forgive."

The organization has proven to be a valuable tool both in working with the city and in addressing issues outside the governmental arena. One such issue is jobs. The area of jobs came into focus as three major supermarkets began building new facilities in our area. The businesses were welcome because the quality of food is substandard in inner-city markets. The Jobs Committee met with the store executives. Armed with the unemployment statistics and an overview of the labor market in the community, the committee made the executives aware of our need for jobs and our willingness to act as an ambassador between the stores and the neighborhood people. SLACO volunteered to set up neighborhood employment offices and assist people in filling out job applications as well as doing initial interviews to screen people. Thus poor people could apply for jobs without spending hours and dollars on public transportation. The process would also help store personnel departments discover the cream of the crop with less time and effort. At first the stores were less than enthusiastic, but finally concessions and agreements were made. The stores conceded to employment offices in churches, set quotas of neighborhood employees, and regular monitoring of continued employment practices. Fairer food prices for quality products would be a long-term advantage for all neighborhood shoppers.

Now that SLACO neighborhoods have become more livable, what is the likelihood that they will become trendy neighborhoods for the new urban gentry? That question defines the problems starting to befall many city neighborhoods where the ethnic and racial minorities are being moved out and replaced by the urban pioneers. Certainly there are many vacant homes and businesses in SLACO neighborhoods. My own belief is that if people of different races and economic status are attracted here, there is room for them. The community would benefit from the diversity. My hope would be that the newcomers are attracted to the community because of the pride SLACO helped to establish and build. In that sense, the newcomers would be attracted by the already present sense of community.

Successful community organizing is people building. Insofar as tangible issues and successful campaigns allow that to happen, great. However, tangible results are not always essential. Just as individuals grow in the face of challenge and difficulties, the same is true of organizations. Conversely, some successes are important, otherwise people become so frustrated they either quit or turn to violence. The point is that successful community organizing develops a spirit of pride and enthusiasm as people see themselves taking control of their own destiny.

One evaluation day our discussion question was: What is the best thing about SLACO? SLACO secretary Claudine Clay answered with a proud smile: "The best thing about SLACO to me is that no one knows how to quit. When we fail, we just back off and re-examine the situation and choose another plan of attack. That's what SLACO taught me about life that I never knew before. Don't quit!"

The testimony of these people and the evidence of their lives made my pastoral decision regarding community work a very satisfying one. Through SLACO I saw lifeless people energized. Jesus said, "I came that you may have life and have it more abundantly."

6

VISITATION COMMUNITY CREDIT UNION

All our money has a moral stamp. It is coined over again in an inward mint. The uses we put it to, the spirit in which we spend it, give it a character which is plainly perceptible to the eye of God.

—Thomas Starr King
English dramatist, 1730-1805

One day about six months after my arrival at Visitation I was called to the door. Instead of the usual person in need, a young man in a three-piece suit and button-down collar stood before me. He said his name and presented me with a card as fast as an F.B.I. man flashes his badge. The card read, "Missouri Division of Credit Unions, Examiner."

"Father, I have to talk to you about the credit union." His dour expression made me yearn for a regular beggar at the door.

I knew that there was a parish credit union that had been founded in 1958, but I was ignorant of any details of the organization. While the questions he proceeded to ask were somewhat vague, his tone of voice warned me to expect trouble. He had already experienced untold frustration trying to track down one of the credit union volunteers; now he had collared me.

The credit union picture looked dismal. Assets were

$120,000. There were about $40,000 in loans; 25 percent of the loans were delinquent. Savings accounts were not insured. The credit union was insolvent. The examiner's proposal was to liquidate the credit union and give each saver 70 cents for each of his or her savings dollars. That would end the examiner's worries — and give me the biggest headache of my young pastorate.

Few things could have happened at the parish in that first year that would have been a greater personal cross for me. I am the son of Philip W. Kleba, a CPA who had devoted much time and energy to the development of credit unions in the state of Missouri. "Credit unions are a practical form of Christian charity," my dad would say. "People save their money together so that they can lend it to their friends and neighbors in time of need." My dad's message conveyed a passion for living the faith through sound financial assistance.

As pastor there was the red-faced embarrassment I felt when I heard the dire story from the auditor. He alleged all types of mismanagement and aloofness on the part of the volunteer board and staff and questioned the integrity of parish members. In addition, the notion of liquidation sent chills up my spine. I realized that as pastor I would get all kinds of questions and criticism from people who had placed their savings in the church credit union. Parishioners would say, "Father, I'm surprised at you. You never should have let this happen." Or they would ask, "Father, is the parish going to repay me for what I lost in the church credit union?"

I also felt bad for the people. It's true that there were no large accounts at the credit union, but a closer look would reveal that although the people wouldn't lose much, for some it was everything they had.

The examiner left with a request that I inform the officers of his visit and urge them to contact him for a very important meeting. As we parted, he turned back to say. "Father, I wish you would try to join us when I meet with the manager and board of the credit union. Maybe there is some way your feel for credit unions would be of assistance to us in facing this problem."

I didn't relish the job of being the messenger who brought

the bad news. However, I contacted the members and told them the story in brief, set up a convenient meeting time and then added the tagline: "If you think there is some way for me to help in this situation, let me know. I'm not a stranger to credit unions. My dad worked with them and believed in them." They promptly invited me to the meeting.

I did a lot of thinking and praying about the matter during the 10 days that elapsed before the meeting. I couldn't speak to many people about the situation. I definitely didn't want to mention it to anyone in the parish because it was confidential. Besides, any rumors would cause a run on the credit union and hasten its collapse. I did talk to my family about the general state of the problem.

"You do what you want," my mom said openly. "But you know what your dad would say. I'm sure some of his friends from the credit union movement are still involved and would be willing to help you."

The fateful meeting was not quite as traumatic as I had anticipated. The examiner was more hopeful than in our earlier private talk. He seemed to warm up to the interested and congenial board and manager. The facts, however, highlighted the grim story of unpaid loans, lack of depositors' insurance and shabby records. The mismanagement resulted primarily from the demands placed on overworked volunteers. To my surprise the meeting ended with a challenge to correct the situation rather than an ultimatum to liquidate the credit union.

Some messages came through clearly. First, the Missouri Division of Credit Unions was unwilling to liquidate the credit union because of the bad publicity that move would generate for all credit unions. Second, there was a willingness on the part of the Visitation board and volunteers to correct the problems. Finally, there was the desire to make the credit union a catalyst in the rebuilding of the community. The closing of the credit union would cause yet another crisis of confidence in the community.

The determination to face the challenge and solve the problems called for a covenant of silence and a commitment of capital to the tottering credit union. The board members could not possibly divulge the shakiness of the credit union without causing a run by depositors. To show their commitment, all of the board members agreed to freeze the money in their savings accounts. Their fortunes, small as they were, were on the line.

The State of Missouri was willing to give us one year to straighten out our books and collect the bad loans. The first task called for long hours of checking and tracing the pen-and-paper trail through several years to correct errors and imbalances. The second task also required herculean efforts. In addition, a program to attract new depositors was begun. This was particularly difficult because the accounts were not insured. The final task was to approach other credit unions in the St. Louis area to ask for guidance and possible financial aid.

Saving the credit union was a vast undertaking and would never have been attempted except for the fact that the area suffered such horrible financial woes. A community-owned alternative economic institution was needed. Yes there were banks, savings and loan associations, and even pawn shops in the community, but none of them made any return to the community. In view of this, the board members set out to move mountains. We would not be satisfied until the credit union qualified for savings insurance to $100,000 from the National Credit Union Administration. In the process of meeting this goal, Visitation Credit Union received enormous help from many sources: Herb Hunter, Don Berra of the Missouri State Credit Union League, Joe Whalen of the Ralston-Purina Credit Union, Floyd Agostinelli of Alternative Economics, Inc., and Paul Boenninghausen, a credit union consultant. Several old friends of my dad also surfaced who were convinced that a good credit union could be a cornerstone of community renewal.

In order to conceptualize the impact that a good credit union can have on a neighborhood, it is vitally important to understand two aspects of micro-economics. First, the difference between a rich neighborhood and a poor neighborhood is more than just the amount of money that is available. The big difference is the question of who *controls* the money in the neighborhood. The second factor is the number of times the same dollar passes through the neighborhood to produce goods and services.

In both rich and poor neighborhoods only a portion of the

money that comes into the community stays there. Everyone has to pay bills for goods and services. Some of that money goes for utilities and may end up in New York or Saudi Arabia. Some goes for housing and insurance and ends up in Hartford or Omaha. Some goes for food, clothing and personal expenses. Finally, some portion of the money is likely to go into savings.

How much of that money in savings is available to people who need to borrow? Not much if we are talking about people in poor communities.

The second economic factor is the number of times that a dollar goes through a community. A person who pays a dollar for house insurance to a company based in another state has spent a dollar that is only likely to come back to the community if there is a fire or other catastrophe. The dollar is spent one time. Another dollar is spent at the local grocery store. That dollar is paid to a clerk who lives in the community. The clerk spends the dollar to get her hair styled at a local shop. The beautician spends the dollar buying cosmetics at a local supply house. The dollar is paid to the salesman who lives in the area. He spends the dollar at a local store. The dollar has been spent and re-spent in the neighborhood six times.

It is conceivable that the dollar could continue to flow in that fashion endlessly. The difference between a rich and poor neighborhood is that a rich neighborhood turns over a dollar about 25 times before it disappears from the community. In a poor neighborhood, the dollar disappears almost immediately. One reason is that there are few quality goods and services available in the inner city. A second factor is that the money deposited in neighborhood banks in poor communities seldom comes back into the area because of restrictive lending policies. Furthermore, poor people only borrow small amounts of money. Small loans cost just as much to process as large loans and consequently are not cost effective. Banks and savings and loan associations prefer to lend their money to pawn shops.

I decided to investigate the pawn shop situation. I knew I could not do it firsthand because the pawnbrokers in the area knew who I was and would give me special treatment. I called Creed Scull, the Visitation maintenance man, to my office and gave him the Helbros self-winding watch my parents had given me for a graduation present.

"Creed, take this watch to the best pawn shop in the neighborhood and borrow as much money on it as you can."

He came back 30 minutes later with a crisp new five-dollar bill!

"This is all I could get," he said, too embarrassed to look at me as he held out the money. Along with it he handed me a pawn ticket. I had never seen one before so I was interested in reading the small print.

"Not responsible for loss due to theft or fire," I read aloud.

"What is the interest rate that I will have to pay when I redeem it?" I asked innocently.

"I don't know," Creed replied. "All I know is what's on the ticket."

"I read the ticket," I protested. "It doesn't say anything about the interest rate."

"The man will tell me when I go back to get it," he stated confidently. "You just have to pay him what he says you owe."

I fumed with disbelief, but I knew the pawnbroker made the rules. This was the tuition I would have to pay for a course in ghetto economics. The watch was pawned on a Monday, and I paid my tuition by redeeming it on Thursday.

I called Creed back to my office and gave him the pawn ticket and a ten-dollar bill. I didn't want to take any chance that the watch would get lost and I would have to explain to my mom. She would never understand pawning my graduation present for five dollars. Once more Creed was back quickly with the merchandise and my change. He had paid $1 interest on a $5 loan over the period of four days. The annual percentage rate was in excess of 1800%. That was unbelievable!

The story to this point demonstrates several things. The Visitation neighborhood was suffering from economic collapse. The credit union, which was supposed to be addressing the problem of the poor neighborhood, was also in a precarious position. The only thing standing between it and forced liquidation by the Missouri Division of Credit Unions was a handful of determined people.

Ed Wortham was one such person. A short man with a shy smile, Ed seemed to be a fixture on the neighborhood streets. Since his retirement about five years earlier, he had stayed active by becoming the newspaper deliveryman for our four-block area. No one in that area was a stranger for Ed, and no favors were too demanding for this active oldster.

"Hi, Father," said Ed as he shuffled over the threshold of the rectory one day. "Do you know me?"

"I know you are the newspaper man, but I don't know your name," I admitted. "I think you live right down the street," I added quickly, so as not to appear too stupid.

"That's right, that's right," he repeated nervously. "My name's Wortham, and I've lived on this street for 27 years. I know everybody here. I've seen a lot of people come and go, and I know 'em all." He cleared his throat, and resumed with halting timidity. "Do you, ah, do you have some kind of a bank or credit union here?" he asked, his eyes never meeting mine.

"Yes, we have a parish credit union," I answered in a matter-of-fact way.

He moved to another subject. "Do you know Barbara Parker, that pretty young lady who just moved in down the street?"

"I think I know her, but not well." I had seen the new woman with the shining ebony hair and full figure, but I didn't want to appear too interested in this lovely new neighbor.

With a disappointed frown marking his brow, he continued. "Did you know that her house was broken into? Someone must have scared the burglar away because nothing was taken, but her house was broken into. It's so sad to see that happen especially to new people who just move into the neighborhood like Ms. Parker. She's such a fine person. I really like her. We need her kind in the neighborhood. I'm sure happy she didn't get hurt. That's one thing I'm happy about." His sentences poured out in hurried tenderness.

"I didn't know about her house, but I too am happy she didn't get hurt or lose anything," I assured him.

"Father, she needs to borrow some money to get new locks on her doors. It's too bad when people need bars on their home, but she needs those too. We need to keep her kind in the neighborhood," he reaffirmed. "She needs to borrow some money from the credit union to repair her house."

"She's the person who will have to take care of that," I informed him. "You can't borrow money for her."

"I want to help her," he reassured me. "I will help her to do what she needs to get a loan. We need her kind in this neighborhood. I don't know if she can afford the work that needs to be done, but she has to be safe in that house."

"How do you intend to help her?" I inquired.

"I'll help her get the loan. I'll co-sign the note. I'll do whatever she needs me to do," he stated flatly.

"If she just moved in, how do you know you want to co-sign a loan for her? If she has debts from just moving in, maybe she can't afford a loan," I cautioned in a ponderous fashion.

"Father, I'm a good judge of people, and I've seen a lot of people in this neighborhood in the years that I've sold newspapers. I know she's a good woman. If she can't afford the loan, I'll have to buy the lock and steel bars for her because I wouldn't like to see her get hurt." His determined seriousness gave way to a more relaxed smile as he looked at me for the first time. "Father, I'm a Christian and I know we have to help our neighbor and that's why I'm here — to help Ms. Parker. I wouldn't forgive myself if she got hurt."

"If you think you want to help her, you'll have to get her to talk to the loan committee of the credit union. I have nothing to do with that part of the credit union. Those are the people who will decide if she will get a loan. That's not in my hands."

"Well, Father, I'll tell you. My credit is good. You ask anybody and they'll tell you that Ed Wortham pays his bills. The *Post* and the *Globe* would like to have a thousand carriers who always deliver the newspapers and get their money paid in on time. Let me ask you, Father, when it snowed two feet, did you get your newspaper?"

"I have to admit, Ed, it was there right on schedule," I replied with the smile of a satisfied customer.

"You just call my bank or call the newspapers and ask them if Ed Wortham's credit good. I don't owe any money to anyone."

"I'm sure that is so, Ed. I think you are a person of impeccable character. It's a pleasure to have you as a neighbor."

Ed went to the basement credit-union office to repeat his story about the importance of Barbara's security and his own top-notch credit rating. After a conversation with the manager to make certain of the loan procedure, he returned.

"This is the form that Ms. Parker will have to fill out in order to borrow the money. She will have to get several bids on the work that she needs to do. I'm sure it will cost hundreds of dollars, but it's important to keep good, new people in the area. I know that I will be able to help her."

He waved goodbye to me with one hand while he stuffed the loan application in his pocket and went down to Barbara's house to give her the details of the loan process.

Barbara got her loan and had her house repaired. Ed co-signed the note. The loan was never on the delinquency list and so almost escaped the attention of everyone. One thing that wasn't so easy to overlook, however, was Ed's eagerness to insure the safety of a new neighbor. Another thing that was obvious was the Christian faith and love that was the undergirding of his kind offer. Ed was not a member of Visitation Church. His eagerness to bear another's burden was the perfect example of the possible ecumenical dimensions of the Visitation Credit Union.

The Board was duly impressed with the soundness of the loan to Barbara. It bore no resemblance to the bad loans that had been made to life-long Visitation parishioners. The next time the question about changing the charter to allow for greater ecumenical participation was raised, the motion passed. Ed's faith had moved mountains. Ed was also the personification of the credit union motto, "Credit unions are for service."

One of the ways in which credit unions offer that service is through education. People who are credit union members must be taught how to use money for service. That type of money management begins close to home with the root definition of economics — management of the household. Good money management must be instilled in credit union members. Credit unions teach economic democracy because each of the members has the right to vote for officers at the annual meeting. The principle is one member, one vote. No preference is given to the larger depositors. Credit unions teach cooperation and challenge people to invest their money in the common community pot. People who invest their money are usually more willing to invest themselves, and as a consequence of that, credit unions teach volunteerism. All of the positions on the board and the committees are held by persons who donate their time and energy. Consequently, credit unions are usually able to keep their costs down and offer better service to ordinary people than other financial institutions.

In 1976 Visitation Credit Union began to ride on the surge that credit unions experienced nationally. The problems that had beset us two years earlier had been solved, and Visitation obtained National Credit Union Association depositor insurance. The credit union was starting to set goals for itself with an eye toward becoming the economic center of the community, a vision that blended well with the vision statement of the parish. Several steps were crucial to making that happen.

The credit union needed to move out of its cramped, dank and inaccessible quarters in the basement of the rectory. Some thought that the previous delinquency rate was actually encouraged by the image of the office which was located adjacent to the emergency food pantry of the St. Vincent de Paul Society. It was too simple for people to equate a loan from the credit union with a "handout" from the St. Vincent de Paul Society. In view of that, we contacted a merchant, Andy Wurm, who had empty office space on a busy commercial strip. His family-run tire business had made a commitment to excellence and service in the area. The unused office was cluttered with junk ranging from hub caps to bar signs and had not been cleaned since Andy had purchased the building.

"Sure, Father, the credit union can use the place. You will have to clean it, decorate it and help pay for the heat. But we ought to be able to work something out. Heck, I might need to use the credit union myself sometime, and then it will be very handy," he said with a beaming smile and a gleam in his eye.

Even before the dollar-a-year lease was signed, the office became a beehive of volunteer cooperation. While office design and furniture were still drawing-board items, members started to haul trash and remove decades of dirt and dust. A local artist designed some graphics for the walls, and the Banks of Ste. Genevieve provided tellers' windows and other furniture. The credit union was undergoing a facelift.

A petition to broaden the field of membership was approved by the Missouri Division of Credit Unions. Visitation Community Credit Union would serve all the people who lived, worked or worshiped within a 15-parish geographic boundary. Our credit union would not be a strictly Catholic operation; it would be open-minded and ecumenical. However, changing the credit union character did not cause people to rush forward and seek membership. The community at large didn't know of our existence.

The new office had a paid manager and, in contrast to our basement office, a window facing the busy world of Kingshighway and Dr. Martin Luther King Drive. The beige walls were highlighted by peach and brown stripes that ran the length of the room near the ceiling. These added movement to the decor and were a cheerful contrast to the drabness of the old office. The salary for the manager was subsidized by several grants from individuals and augmented by a larger grant from the Missouri Credit Union League.

On February 17, 1958 the Visitation pastor, Father Art Peet, and 11 parish members had pooled their savings and obtained a charter. Eighteen years later the faith and commitment of those twelve continued to generate expanded life and hope. We had been faithful to their original vision, but we were also open to its evolution in the present. Two dramatic changes that ushered us into the new era of credit unions had not been available in 1958. They were share insurance on the savings of the members and the more inclusive community credit union status. Twelve members with a dream and $5 each had led the way. In the church there is something formidable about 12 people who risk.

Although the credit union development under paid manager Wayman Revere was significant, growth was not dramatic. We had an office that gave the appearance of a business, but we also had some old problems and a few new ones. One of the old problems was that we had the image of a paper-and-pencil operation in the age of computers. Another was the small profit margin and the small amount of interest paid on savings.

The new problems revolved around the lack of security and the atmosphere of fear that permeated that busy intersection. Andy Wurm Tire Company had two German shepherd guard dogs. The credit union had an electronic lock. The manager had to press a buzzer whenever a new person appeared at the door. The credit union was intent on broadening its membership, but afraid that any new person who came in might be a robber. The neighborhood had very limited parking, and many members were leery about their safety as pedestrians leaving a financial office. The building next door was a raucous bar that frequently had undesirable characters loitering by the door.

Any grandiose illusions of instant success vanished like smoke, and the daily grind began. Each of our services required added patience and personal attention to people with limited educations and little expertise about money matters. We had stuck out our neck, and we were moving in tortoise fashion. The fact that the physical move was not an instant answer caused a certain loss of motivation and drive. Maybe this wasn't the good idea that it had been perceived to be by many members. Yet whenever there was some indication of willingness to throw in the towel, a new opportunity presented itself.

One such opportunity was the vacant Sears Building about one-half block south on Kingshighway. Sears had turned the building over to the Urban League to develop into a community services building. In the enormous floor space there was one area just right for the credit union. It had been the credit office of the Sears store. There were tellers windows, cash drawers and several large safes. It was not the type of office space that would be attractive to many other groups, but it was just what Visitation Community Credit Union needed. We approached Sears with a plan to rent the space through an agreement under the auspices of the Neighborhood Assistance Act. The Act allowed corporations to make specific contributions to community groups and get increased corporate tax breaks. We worked out a plan whereby the credit union would get a five-year lease on this space for $200 monthly. Thus in

1978 the credit union moved to our present air-conditioned credit union office.

Soon it was time to enter the computer era. The credit union manager at this time was Daryl Casey, a young, idealistic graduate fresh out of St. Louis University. He was not a person who would punch out after a mere eight hours of work. While Daryl prepared the accounts for data processing, he continued to serve the members and promoted the growth of the operation. Slowly and steadily he moved the credit union into the computer age. Fortunately, he did not have to do the job alone.

One of the long-time supporters of the Visitation effort was Don Berra. During the struggle for survival this suave, gentle Italian worked with the Missouri State Credit Union League. At that time he generously encouraged and tirelessly pushed us over the insolvency hurdle. He left that position and in 1979 was the manager of the sizable First Community Credit Union. He had regularly stayed in touch and supported our uneven growth. Now he was heading the largest credit union in the state.

Don was in his 40s. He had grown up with the credit union movement. Don knew the history of our small, struggling credit union, and always remembered the spirit of cooperation that distinguishes the credit union movement from the banking business. When we discussed our need to computerize the office, he was very encouraging and eager to make his contribution. He worked with us to decide the exact date when the credit union would be keyed into the League Data Center. He helped us organize the internal chores that had to be done. When some last-minute tidying up was necessary, he sent several of his staff to work with us to see that everything was in perfect order. His professional help assured that we would not be plagued in the future by the computer horror, "Garbage in, garbage out."

Data processing for the Visitation Community Credit Union represented a quantum leap into the modern world. The year was drawing to a close, the task had been completed, and now it was time to celebrate this remarkable achievement. As the treasurer of the credit union, it was my privilege to present

Daryl with a small Christmas bonus to thank him for his commitment to the credit union. I was proud to make the presentation, but embarrassed by the paltry gift of a few hundred dollars. On December 23, I approached Daryl and interrupted his work at the office.

"Daryl," I began timidly, "it's my pleasure and my embarrassment to present you with this Christmas bonus. You know that the credit union is still struggling. Hence, you know best of all that this gift is a big percentage of our profits. In those terms you may be receiving one of the biggest Christmas bonuses distributed in the entire city of St. Louis this year. However, in real dollars the amount is insignificant. Please accept it as a token of our great appreciation and esteem for you as a person of wonderful integrity and tireless, unrelenting generosity."

Daryl accepted the check with a warm smile and sparkling eyes. In his deep resonant voice, he responded sincerely. "Father, I really appreciate this gift. And I understand all the sentiments behind it. Let me assure you that I knew what I was getting into when I took this job. I have classmates who graduated from St. Louis University who are working for some of the biggest banks and businesses in the country. And here I am working for one of the smallest credit unions. But some of them are mere tokens. Father, here I'm the boss. I get to make decisions, and I implement new policies. I'm somebody."

He continued, "Father, I was born, raised and educated in this neighborhood. My parents always told us that we don't just get what we can and then get out. We are to return to the community what we have received from it. We are to make it better for the generation that comes up behind us. So please don't apologize for the Christmas bonus. I'm thrilled to be remembered and I'm flattered with all that trust that you have placed in me."

Then he embarrassed me by adding, "Father, it's easy to be generous when I see just how generous and committed you are. Merry Christmas to you, too."

With an outstanding manager and data processing, the credit union was able to make some assaults on inner-city blight. And, during this period, it loaned money to Jerry and Carmele Hall. Jerry is in middle management at Bell Telephone and Carmele is the principal of Bishop Healy School. Both of them have roots and family in the heart of the city and their parents continue to live in those ancestoral neighborhoods. The Halls wanted to return to the city so their son Jason could grow up near his grandparents, and also so they could make their personal contribution to stemming the brain drain that afflicts the inner city. One of the detriments to family life and child rearing in a poor neighborhood is that the children see very few heroes and adult role models. The absence of role models has a devastating effect on the self-image of minority children.

Jerry and Carmele bought a dilapidated, three-story house that still maintained some stateliness in its stone facade and bay windows. While the purchase was a bargain, they knew they were in for years of hard work and the investment of money, energy and time. They approached three neighborhood banks for a home-improvement loan. Each of the banks wanted to do business with the Halls, but not in the central city. Consequently, Jerry and Carmele came to the Visitation Community Credit Union for several loans. One was for a roof and thermopane windows; another for new plumbing and a modern bathroom; another for a new back porch and second-floor sun deck. Each of these loans has been solid from the credit union standpoint.

The record of the Visitation Community Credit Union has been an invitation for banks to get back into the business of serving the needs of the people. The first bank to see the value of the credit union and recognize some responsibility to the community that it calls home was Cass Bank in downtown St. Louis. City Bank and Mark Twain Bankshares have also been supportive and encouraging.

Many of our social programs, including the credit union, received support because of my involvement with retreat programs. The retreat ministry put me into a setting where people were open to taking a serious look at their lives. These people usually found themselves comfortably well-off. They came content in body, but hungry in spirit. This was refreshing for me because the material demands of ministry with the poor can be very tiring. They can be even more taxing if there are few resources available to help needy people. Consequently, I gave several retreats each year.

With surprising frequency people step forward in these retreats who are eager and interested in working with the poor. I am surprised that this surprises me anymore. When people discover God who is love in their life, they are more willing and able to reach out in love to others. Some people need material goods; all people need God.

It was the middle of 1984 before Visitation Community Credit Union surpassed the million dollar mark. By this time we had become so accustomed to slow, steady progress that the achievement almost went by unnoticed. However that milestone allowed the credit union to look at another important area of service, the addition of share drafts, the interest-bearing checking accounts of the credit union world. Steps in that direction were taken under the leadership of another committed manager, Jack Marsh. Jack had come out of a community organizing background and was a good liaison with SLACO. He had apprenticed under Daryl.

With our financial growth and computerized technical efficiency, Jack began the move into share drafts. This cost-free checking service filled one of the last big gaps that continued to exist in the credit union efforts to service the everyday needs of the average member. Finally, we could tell our members, "Kiss your banker goodbye."

Visitation Community Credit Union, in its faltering but consistent growth, has been a liberating influence on the community. Individuals have been helped, money has been used to leverage power and respect; and unyielding institutions have been challenged and slightly changed. At the heart of this effort has been the awareness that our God calls us to communal justice. The attainment of that end requires the refashioning of structures. It is the third dynamic of relational theology. The first notion is plain enough. We must love God—the intrapersonal dimension of theology. The second notion is we must love our neighbor as ourself—the interpersonal dimension of theology. Only recently has the third dimension of theology, the societal dimension, begun to be regarded as intrinsically related to the spiritual life. We must build human solidarity. That dimension is the role that the credit union tries to address in our community. Once we understand that there is a Christian approach to money, the next step is to understand that there is a Christian approach to economic institutions and structures. Or, in Martin Luther King, Jr.'s words:

> The dispossessed of this nation—the poor, both white and Negro—live in a cruelly unjust society, therefore, they must organize a revolution against that injustice, not against the lives of their fellow citizens, but against the structures through which the society is refusing to lift the load of poverty.

7

HOUSING BUILT ON HOPE

Home is the place where, when you have to go there, They have to take you in.

— Robert Frost

Home is where the heart is.

— Pliny the Elder

Holy Thursday is hardly the time for a priest to accompany an old woman to the hospital. On second thought, maybe it is. It is a way to "wash the feet" of another as Jesus did on that first Holy Thursday. Little did I know when I took Evelyn to the hospital that her condition would become critical and I would spend hours there. Even less did I suspect that her 90-year-old mother would become an added burden. And least of all did I guess that I would eventually buy Evelyn's house.

Evelyn Jones lived across the street, just 50 yards west of church. The rumor in the neighborhood was that she was a crabby recluse; the truth was that she was a visually-impaired person who was lonesome and fear-filled. Evelyn's vision problem caused her to suffer from blurriness and a horrible glare in even moderate light. Consequently, she usually stayed closed in behind drawn curtains or, on the rare occasion that she did show her face, with her eyes hidden behind dark glasses. Neighborhood kids feared her rare appearances and eerie look.

It was the classic situation where children whisper, "That house is haunted and a witch lives there."

The house was a two-story, two-family flat. The upstairs had been vacant since her husband's death. The red brick structure with the white trim and stone window sills was slipping into decay. The front steps and concrete sidewalk were cracked, chipped and crumbling.

Evelyn's husband had been an energetic and highly successful person. He had been in charge of all the restrooms and shoeshine stands in the Chase-Park Plaza Hotel. The average person who tips the towel man at a fine hotel never realizes how much money circulates through those rooms. For over 35 years Mr. Jones had operated these concessions and received a percentage of all the tips. Mr. Jones' income was considerable, and he and his wife never spent it on extravagant living or impulse buying. Their lifestyle as a childless couple was as predictable as the water that ran from the golden spigots in the Chase-Park Plaza restrooms. The Joneses were good at tucking away nest eggs.

Despite the headaches of taking care of an oversized and under-used old house, Evelyn tried to maintain it after her husband's death according to her capabilities and needs. One of the things she did was paint the living room a dark, almost black green so that the bright glare from the large windows would be lessened. But it takes a lot of repairing to maintain an old house. In Evelyn's case most of those repairs never got done because she never noticed that they were needed. But to Evelyn the old place was home; she owned it.

Holy Week at the hospital with Evelyn and her mother Velma was an authentic religious experience. The connection of the suffering and death of Jesus and the suffering of a follower of Jesus was obvious. Evelyn was reconciled with the church and very much at peace in spirit despite her physical condition. Her usual poor state of health had been further undermined by a case of flu that lingered and sapped her strength. In one of those ironies of life, 90-year-old Velma was much healthier than Evelyn, her 60-year-old daughter.

One of her immediate concerns was caring for her mail and her bills. She had gotten behind because of her sickness and had seldom been very current anyway due to her vision problems. She gave me the key to her house and told me where to find the bills and the checkbook. She asked that I get things organized and then bring the checks to the hospital for her signature. I was happy to do that. My previous work as a hospital chaplain had taught me that relief from daily worries and anxieties is an important part of the healing process. Watching her house and paying the bills was simple.

One of the surprises in writing her checks was discovering her staggering wealth. Jetsetters and oil tycoons may have $100,000 balances in their checking accounts, but not the average inner-city resident. I had a hard time believing my eyes when I saw the balance in the book, so I went to the bank to inquire. The banker verified the balance. Writing checks on Evelyn's account proved much easier than paying the church bills.

By the end of Easter Week, Evelyn had improved dramatically. She was ready to make the decision to move to a senior-citizen apartment and leave her old house. She wanted parishioners to help her move her furniture.

One day after we had diagramed the furniture placement in her new apartment, she said, "I want you to buy my house from me so that I don't have to worry about that place anymore."

I was flabbergasted! We had never talked about disposing of the old house. I knew one thing. I didn't need a two-family house across the street from my enormous rectory. "Why would you ever want to sell me the house?" I asked innocently.

"You'll take care of it and you'll get good people to live there," she complimented.

I knew what she was saying. She wanted to know that the house would get good care in the same way that a person who gives away puppies wants to make sure they will have a good home. But I also knew I didn't need another building. On the other hand, I *did* need a building as a "classroom" for students in the CETA Program who were interested in learning home repairs. The Comprehensive Employment Training Act would pay people to do jobs and develop job skills. The problem in the home repair aspect of the law was that workers were never allowed to do interior work. The intent of the law was to safeguard the privacy and security of the elderly by never allowing these chronically unemployed CETA workers into their homes. While the intent of the law was laudable, the practice was detrimental to the CETA workers' learning. Exterior repair work allowed people to learn some carpentry, cement work, painting and tuckpointing. However, the real guts of the house were not accessible to them. At that time Brothers United, Inc., a home repair corporation headed by Brother Gene Garcia, S.J., had several young men in training under very skillful supervision. For them, the CETA law was a great frustration. It had never occurred to me before that owning a dilapidated home would be a real blessing. But now I saw Evelyn's home as a laboratory for Brothers United. It was a place to "bend the rule."

I pursued the conversation with Evelyn to determine a fair price for the house and wondered aloud if some of her family members might not be unhappy to have me purchase it. She was ready to sell for a give-away price of $2,600. I was interested, but I mentioned my concern about possible family objections. "I want you to buy the house," she insisted.

"I think that you ought to wait until you start to feel better and get out of here. You're not well enough to make a decision of this gravity. We'll talk after you're well," I assured her.

"The sooner I'm rid of that house, the quicker I'll get well," she retorted. "You get the papers drawn up this week, and I'll sign them right here in the hospital." Her voice got stronger with each syllable.

I whined and said, "I don't feel right about this. The nurses will think I'm a gigolo. Nobody sells a house to the priest who brought her to the hospital. We better wait, I just don't feel right about this."

The ball was back in her court, and she didn't miss the volley.

"I'm going to sell that house this week, and you just get somebody to do the paperwork for us. Let them think you're a gigolo. I don't care."

Her final statement left me with no doubt. Gigolo or not, I was to buy the house. I knew that there was no better possibility for Brothers United. I talked to Marie Herndon, a notary, to ask her if she could witness the signing. I talked to Robert Harding, a realtor and credit union officer, to see if he would be able to draw up the necessary sale papers. Everyone was most eager to help, but first they had to listen to me explain the background of this transaction. I was deeply concerned that no one perceive me as a con artist hidden behind a Roman collar.

We went to the hospital on Tuesday afternoon. Before any of the papers were taken from the briefcase, I explained to the private duty nurse who all of us were. After she understood the nature of the business, I asked the nurse if she would question Evelyn about her desire to sell the house. When she gave a strongly affirmative answer, the sale was completed in a few minutes. Evelyn was relieved and happy and on the road to recovery.

I had a house that I personally didn't need. But the community needed the house because the Brothers United needed a place to practice their skills. When the work was complete, I sold the house to a young couple. Their purchase became the first Visitation Community Credit Union mortgage loan. Other houses were bought and/or improved by Brothers United, Inc. The lives of a few families were changed. Finally the challenge of a large project presented itself. To my surprise, it wasn't even in Visitation parish.

Our neighboring parish, St. Mark's, had been haunted for about six years with a vacant, dilapidated apartment building. The yellow brick building with the carved stone lintels was merely the shadow of a bygone era of stately grace and a tree-lined avenue. Now it was a two-story monstrosity which attracted derelicts and winos. Sadly, the building fronted on the De Porres Consolidated School. Realizing the horrendous image it presented, some imaginative St. Mark's people decided to look into the purchase of the building. The cost would be about $8,500 for back taxes and the foreclosed mortgage. That was far more than any of the members wanted to invest in an eyesore.

Two members of the parish staff, Father Rich Creason and Sister Dorothy Cox, were convinced something good could happen to that building. If not, it could be demolished and the investment recouped through the sale of antique bricks. Rich mentioned this dream to Dan and Mary Lee Henroid in a friendly conversation. A short while after the discussion the Henroids inherited some money from an aunt. Since it was a windfall, they thought they could afford to risk it without endangering the family budget. And so, the Academy Community Center Inc. was begun with the purchase of this hapless building and the investment of a faith-filled young family. For 30 months the building stood without any type of improvement. The only thing new about the building was the name on the title and an expensive, hard-to-purchase insurance policy. Yet the board members of Academy Community Center, many of them St. Mark's parishioners, had a vision of something beautiful across from De Porres School.

About that time I was having dinner with the leadership team of the Sisters of St. Mary, a community committed to health care. The Sisters mentioned a new awareness. "We realize that an investment in good housing is an investment in good health care," the treasurer said. "We wish some St. Louis group would do an innovative housing program. Since there is none, we invest our money in the Jubilee Housing Corporation in Washington, D.C."

I asked the Sisters if they had ever heard of the apartment house owned by the Academy Community Center.

They replied, "We haven't but we are very interested in something closer to St. Louis."

As a result of that simple comment, a meeting was planned with the Sisters which later led to a partnership and a $300,000 investment.

Now, with solid financial backing, A.C.C. was able to approach the St. Louis Housing Authority for commitments from the Section 8 Program that would allow rent subsidies for low-income people to live in the apartments. They were also able to apply for a $200,000 grant from the Community Development Agency for federal revenue-sharing funds. Months passed and all the corporate housing technicalities got more and more confusing. The plans for the building had to be redrawn and revised, and it was clear that the funding was still about $80,000 short of what was needed. Throughout this time the building continued to deteriorate under the ice and snow of a terrible winter. In the midst of this confusion Jerry King stepped forward. A very committed developer of City Equity Corporation, Jerry had been a long-time supporter of many endeavors in the area of justice and peace in the St. Louis community. He and his company shared a vision of working to house the poor in St. Louis. With his expertise and never-say-die attitude, A.C.C. was able to find another partner to give life to the dream, a wealthy person who would get a tax shelter through a real-estate investment. Typically, wealthy people look for real-estate deals in Vail, Colorado, Cape Cod or West Palm Beach. However, the same benefits are available in projects like A.C.C., but most shy away fearing that housing for the poor will be mismanaged and not remain habitable long enough to pay off the mortgage. In this regard church and community support are invaluable in order to maintain a quality project.

With the financing solidly in place, the actual work began. Despite a terrible winter with two feet of snow in one weekend, the building was ready in record time. There was less vandalism than the contractor usually experienced in suburbia! After a joyful ribbon-cutting and public blessing, nine family units and four senior-citizen apartments were opened.

The subsidized housing provided for low-income people through the Academy Community Center Corporation became possible through the cooperation of a private developer, a community group, benevolent investors and government agencies. This is an ideal situation. The developer brings expertise, the community group brings credibility and stability, the investors bring dollars (and some gain tax advantages) and the government brings the subsidies that make decent housing for the poor affordable. Other projects that I will discuss were financed in other ways. However, all had community support and government subsidies.

I strongly believe that decent housing is a human right which the church as a primary community builder must support and encourage. The right to decent housing challenges the church to be a prophetic, social conscience. Thus with the completion and occupancy of the Academy Gardens Apartments, I thought, "Surely church people are not above some healthy competition." I took a picture of the empty Holy Ghost School and the lovely new apartments at Academy Gardens. Then I called the provincial of the Sisters of Mercy, another group of religious women in health care in St. Louis. I told Sister Mary Roch that I would like to come and talk with her about the possibilities in inner-city housing. I made it quite clear that the community would be invited to participate in a program similar to the one that the Sisters of St. Mary had found such an excellent investment. Sister invited me to lunch. I took the two contrasting photos and a two-page proposal.

After lunch Sister looked at the pictures and the proposal with considerable interest. The request was for a low-interest investment of $250,000. She said she would discuss this with the people on the leadership team and answer in a short time.

In two weeks Sister Roch wrote that the Sisters of Mercy were happy to be invited into "this excellent project in the inner city." They would commit themselves to a $50,000 no-strings grant to get the project on the drawing boards. When the project was ready to go, they would invest $150,000.

I was ecstatic! Never did I expect such an immediate and sizable gift and commitment. And, during the two-week wait I met Connie Greene. In the course of conversation she mentioned that she had frequently helped at her husband's architectural firm, and I asked if he had ever done any rehabilitation work on turn-of-the-century buildings. She replied, "He rehabed the school of the Academy of the Sacred Heart in St. Charles, Missouri." I asked her if he might be interested in creating apartments out of an old vacant school building. She replied, "You'd have to talk with Peter. Call him."

While the Sisters of Mercy were still pondering their possible commitment, Peter Greene came to visit Holy Ghost School and the adjacent rectory. He was impressed with the large, well-constructed brick buildings. Even though he was fully aware that any architect's fee would be contingent upon adequate funding for the project, he said he would start to do some preliminary drawings. Peter's drawings were more important than the money at this point because most potential investors are scared by the inner city. A drawing of a beautiful building would get them thinking in a positive fashion.

Peter Greene worked on the project, and the Sisters of Mercy sent us a commitment letter. Peter and I went to the St. Louis Housing Authority. This was the simple message we brought. "We have two buildings, we have $200,000, we are as creditable as the Catholic church. Can you help us?"

Several months went by with many maybes and negatives. "There are no Section 8 subsidies." "There is no money." Still Peter kept drawing, Visitation Parish Family and friends kept praying, and everyone looked for a ray of hope at the St. Louis Housing Authority.

A glimmer came in the form of a headline in the *St. Louis Globe Democrat* in late August 1982. The story reported that the St. Louis Housing Authority had $9 million unspent that had to be allocated for some programs or be returned to Washington. Here in St. Louis, Missouri, a city the *Washington Post* had called the "fastest dying city in America," the Housing Authority was sitting on $9 million. It was time to go to work on the politicians. We wrote letters and made telephone calls to Senators Danforth and Eagleton. Marie Herndon, the parish organist, was a friend of Congressman Bill Clay. She arranged an appointment with him.

Marie Herndon, Fred Rogers, the president of SLACO, Gloria Henry and I went to meet with Congressman Clay. We carried the proposed plan for the apartment and the letter of commitment from the Sisters. Certainly, there had to be a way to parlay the letter and the buildings into subsidized apartments. And, the Housing authority had to spend $9 million. He assured us that there was a way. In fact, he thought that our plans were so good that we wouldn't need the money from the Sisters. Rather, the Housing Authority would purchase and rehab the school according to the plans of Peter Greene. Peter would be paid for his work, a fine reward for a job he had begun in faith. Congressman Clay called Housing Authority during our meeting to get the ball rolling. The prayers and the lobbying were working.

Promises from senators and congressmen are encouraging, but it is still a long, hard task to get the bureaucracy to function. After all of his promises, Congressman Clay said, "Don't forget to get the support of Senator Danforth. After all, the Republicans are in power in Washington, you know."

The truth was clear. Danforth had never been to one of our neighborhood meetings, and poor black communities are not places where Republican senators usually get votes. In the search for an opening to Danforth, I called Peter Benoist, a SLACO friend and bank president. "We need some Republican help to develop some housing. How do we get to Senator Danforth?" I asked.

Instantly Peter Benoist responded, "The treasurer of Senator Danforth's election committee is a board member of this bank. He always told us that Danforth wanted to know how he could help." Peter tracked the man down in Minneapolis Airport, and he said he would get "hot on the trail."

September 30, 1982 came and went and there was no word. That had been the deadline on the $9 million. The plans and the purchase agreement and the budget for the project had been presented to the St. Louis Housing Authority. Once more, we called on all the saints and all the politicians we could muster to help us. The word we got was, "Wait"; there had been a 90-day extension granted. Since Congressman Clay was convinced that the Housing Authority would do the school building with 100 percent government funds, we still had the $200,000 from the Sisters of Mercy to consider.

In the shadow of the school was the enormous Holy Ghost Rectory—three stories, 25 rooms and a complete basement. Most of the people of the area were senior citizens. They wanted some senior apartments so they would feel more secure and be able to sell homes which were too large and expensive to maintain. Six months earlier on our first visit to the Housing Authority, the word had slipped out that there were several available slots for Section 8 apartments for senior citizens.

Peter and I went to the St. Louis Housing Authority with new plans to convert the huge, red-brick rectory into a senior citizen apartment building. We were told that in view of Reagan housing cutbacks, the subsidies would only be for three years. That would never be good enough to pay off the construction loan and twenty-year mortgage on the building. However, with the enormous commitment of the Sisters of Mercy, I thought the Archdiocese of St. Louis might also be interested.

The Archdiocese of St. Louis, through a separate corporation called the Cardinal Ritter Institute, operates more housing for the elderly than anyone in Missouri. Cardinal Ritter Institute even manages some of the senior apartments owned by the government. The director of the Cardinal Ritter Institute is committed, soft-spoken, impeccably-dressed Jack Lally. This trim, angular professional taught me social work in the college seminary. It would be no problem getting an appointment with Jack. He was always open to hearing new ideas for helping people.

With a cylinder of blueprints under his arm, Peter accompanied me to Jack's office. Jack was very congenial and fascinated by our presentation. He agreed that the apartments were attractive, but pointed out that they were walk-ups and that an elevator was too costly for such a small building. The subsidy from the Sisters was fine, but we would need an extra $100,000 to do the job. The cost of the building, which the parish intended to sell to the Cardinal Ritter Institute for $1, was fine, but the Section 8 subsidy was only for three years. The building would have a 20-year mortgage when completed. "It would be nice, but the financing is impossible," Jack concluded.

One by one, we tried to refute his objections. Yes, some apartments were on the third floor. However, many poor and elderly people now live in unsanitary, firetrap apartments on the third floor. They would be happy to have a safe, clean, modern walk-up. Yes, the entire project would cost more than $200,000, but there was a possibility of obtaining the rest of the money from the city in a Community Development Block Grant. The money wouldn't have to be repaid, and so the mortgage would be less of a problem. But there was still one insurmountable objection. The mortgage could not be repaid, because the government rent subsidy was only guaranteed for three years. It would not support a 20-year mortgage. The funding was inadequate.

I wondered just how many of the hundreds of units of elderly housing owned by Cardinal Ritter Institute were in the same precarious financial situation, so I asked, "Jack, what is the financial status of the other housing built and owned by Cardinal Ritter Institute?"

With a serious look he replied, "Father, this would be the first building that Cardinal Ritter Institute developed that wasn't totally insured through various government programs."

I shook my head in disbelief. "Are you telling me that every stick of housing built and owned by the Cardinal Ritter Institute is so safe that it would have been financed by a Wall Street banker?"

"That's right," he nodded.

Then I knew it was time to challenge the church. I wrote a letter to Archbishop John L. May. He had been in Chicago and in Mobile and knew urban and rural poverty in the North and South. I tried to analyze the problem. I discussed the letter with people at the parish, and weighed it with others who shared my dream. What if the diocese defaulted on the payment to the Sisters of Mercy? Would they foreclose or declare bankruptcy? What if the subsidy ran out, and the diocese could not afford the expense of running the building? Would they have to turn off the heat or throw the elderly out into the snow? No matter how I asked myself these questions, I always was certain that the Catholic community would never allow any of these dread things to happen. God's people were too good for us even to worry about these situations. If all the past housing commitments had been as financially solid as they were structurally sound, then in a way they had been done without even addressing the gospel mandate of sheltering the homeless.

So I wrote to the archbishop asking for his opinion regarding the possible purchase, rehab and operation of the Holy Ghost Rectory as senior citizen apartments. He wrote back, "If the Sisters are willing to finance it given the questionable situation and the Community Development Authority is willing to make a grant to pay the remainder of the construction cost, then the Cardinal Ritter Institute should purchase the building and move on the opportunity with trust that God will bless everyone involved." I delighted in the reassurance that the church would still accept the challenge to "walk on water." At no time did I think that Cardinal Ritter Institute should risk the future security of its elderly tenants by operating with fiscal irresponsibility. No, that would not be Christian. But, I did think they might take a chance with 11 apartments. We ask more faith of parishioners whom we constantly tell to donate and sacrifice. Yes, they may be out of work or have sick children. They have house or rent payments. But we tell them of the joy of giving and promise them that God is never outdone in generosity. Certainly, the church must also hear that promise.

And so in papers and letters, in blueprints and in the hearts of the Visitation Parish Family, the project was taking shape. However, the Washington HUD connection had still never given the green light for the family apartments at Holy Ghost School.

1983 came, Mardi Gras, Lent, Holy Week, but still no definite word. Then one of the problems surfaced. The architect who was reviewing our plans was unhappy because Peter had proceeded so far without preliminary approval. Our eagerness to move forward had become a roadblock. The Housing Authority architect assigned to our building wanted to dismantle all the plans and only allow Peter to proceed at the bureaucratic pace.

On the Friday after Easter, Peter was ready to joust with the Housing Authority. This time he was going to try to get them all into the same room and demand written documentation for every needed design change. The parish united in prayer. God's grace spilled on everyone in abundance that day. The corrections demanded were less extensive than Peter anticipated. Maybe the criticism was less abrasive or he was just less defensive about the excellence of his drawings. Whatever, he came away from the meeting with renewed determination to meet the next deadline and complete the project.

The deadline was met and the machinery of government went to work one more time to give final approval to the project and refigure all the construction costs. Happily, the project would come in under budget. And, finally, in late June of 1983 the call came from the St. Louis Housing Authority asking me to contact the Archdiocesan attorney. Could he draw up the papers for the sale of the property within two weeks?

In total, over $1,500,000 worth of housing for the poor and elderly was constructed because Dan and Mary Lee were willing to risk their inheritance. Their investment was returned by the Academy Community Center, Inc. Dan and Mary Lee brought their older children to the Open House at the apartments, and they were able to show their children the fruits of lives lived by faith. It's a lesson that can never be learned too early and must be learned close to home.

8

COMMUNITY PRAYER LIFE

Racism is Man's gravest threat to man—the maximum of hatred for a minimum of reason.

—Rabbi Abraham Heuschel

The liturgy inspires the faithful to become of one heart in love.

—*Constitution on the Sacred Liturgy*, No. 10

On January 15, 1984, the birthday of Dr. Martin Luther King, Jr., was marked by a diocesan celebration at the St. Louis Cathedral. The cathedral is a Byzantine masterpiece, but despite the somewhat cold hardness of this type of architecture, the building has always had a warm spot in my heart. My uncle, Monsignor Nicholas W. Brinkman, had been stationed there as his only assignment for over three decades. He died in 1952 after having been responsible for much of the building at this elegant edifice.

On this particular day, an extra glow came from pride as the Rev. Mr. James Herman, deacon from Visitation Parish, was the deacon at the Mass. He proclaimed the Good News from high up in the ornate pulpit. When he concluded the reading, everyone in the vast assembly applauded enthusiastically. It was overwhelming. I was told later that the applause was a greeting for Father Terry Steib, the preacher ascending the pulpit, who was about to become the first black bishop of St. Louis. I was hardly interested in the truth of the matter.

From my perspective all the applause was for James Herman, a St. Louis Street Department employee and a very generous deacon at Visitation.

James' diaconate ordination was the event I most longed for and prayed for as pastor of Visitation. In view of the fierce and unrelenting racism that plagued black Catholics, I felt it was too much to hope for the ordination of a priest. But the ordination of a deacon would be a memorable milestone. Thus the ordination of James Herman in January 1982 was a *cause célèbre*. As I witnessed the ceremony I experienced a certain inner urge to say with Simeon, "Now, Lord, you can dismiss your servant in peace, just as you promised."

In order to appreciate my reaction, you have to know something about racism in the church of St. Louis. Visitation Parish had the first integrated school in the state of Missouri in 1946. Shortly thereafter Joseph Cardinal Ritter became bishop. He was in the forefront of the integration issue in every area of church and civic life. However the hurts have been so deep and the centuries of ugly injustice so brutal that it is difficult for many blacks to see the loving Jesus in the Catholic Church.

Occasionally someone asks, "Why aren't there more black priests and sisters?" Robert L. Robinson of the National Black Catholic Lay Caucus provides an answer:

> In my childhood, Catholic churches were segregated. All of them. They had balconies for the blacks, or a few separate pews in the back of church for blacks. Then, Black Catholic youngsters who wished to become priests had two choices: Africa and Bay St. Louis, Mississippi. Not many could afford Africa and not many dared risk Bay St. Louis. Not many became priests.

Even later, when integration came, black and white altar boys could not serve Mass together. When blacks served Mass, some priests publicly washed their hands at communion to reassure white Catholics that priestly hands had not touched black lips before serving them the Lord's Supper. And, the rank and file of black parishioners had to wait to approach the communion rail until all of the whites in the congregation had been served. Although these practices are in the past, the reality of Catholic church racism has been etched forever in the black psyche.

In 1968 the Caucus of Black Catholic Clergy was organized in Detroit. They boldly stated that the Catholic church in the United States is primarily a racist institution. The Catholic bishops were not pleased with this forthright remark and made no immediate response. Over 10 years later, in 1979, the American bishops issued a pastoral letter on racism entitled *Brothers and Sisters to Us*. This letter stated:

> The structures of our society are subtly racist, for these structures reflect the values which society upholds. They are geared to the success of the majority and the failure of the minority; and members of both groups give unwitting approval by accepting things as they are. Perhaps no single individual is to blame. The sinfulness is often anonymous, but nonetheless real.

Even as Visitation Parish Family was striving to address the larger community in ways already described, a whole process of inner renewal was taking place. Prayer and planning heightened the bonding that would make Visitation a parish family. In line with a desire for liturgical celebrations, Mondays took on a new importance. Monday was the day of the weekly staff meeting. For opening prayer we prepared the liturgy for the coming Sunday. We augmented the staff with interested parishioners who were willing to give their time. First we read through the Sunday readings and shared prayer. Next we tried to be conscious of liturgical seasons, civic celebrations and larger issues of justice. The question before us was the same one that the liturgy committee struggled with in planning for the major feasts: What is the tie-in and flow that exists between daily life and liturgy in the sanctuary?

We formulated the following guidelines for liturgies. We found them life-giving.

1. In selecting persons to serve in various ministries, there should be a fair representation by age, sex, race, economic background and other strata.

2. In view of the growing shortage of priests, there should be as few extra liturgies as possible.

3. When the priest is absent and there is no daily Mass,

the eucharistic ministers should fill in with a service based on the daily scripture readings. After the readings there should be a dialogue homily, prayers of the faithful, the Lord's Prayer and a communion service.

4. The celebrant should always select the options that maximize the participation of the people. Each service should have petitions and time to share a meaningful sign of peace.

5. Especially at the time of holy communion the celebrant himself should be a sign of Jesus' humility. The priest should hold the chalice sometimes rather than the consecrated bread. This would highlight the ministry of the cup and probably influence some Catholics to better value Jesus' presence in the consecrated wine.

There are also other aspects of expression which play an important part in liturgy—singing and dancing. My experience leads me to say that black people are sacramental people. As Father Giles Conwill, the director of vocations for the National Office for Black Catholics, stated:

> Sociologists and anthropologists attest to the fact that there is a distinct Afro-American culture and subcultures. Survivals of African culture are found in many aspects of black life. The most noticeable characteristics occur in areas of family life, music, dancing and religious worship. Our Afro music's concentration on the tympanic beat of the drum and the consequent attention to driving rhythm hearkens back to West Africa . . .
>
> The way black Christians sing the spirituals and the gospels; the choir dance steps used (swaying from side to side—a survival of the trance-induced dancing that readied one for "possession" by the Spirit); the lead singing and groups response in alternation seen in plantation work songs and church songs; all are African in origin. Our African roots are indeed still alive, and the flowering of the various facets of black culture throughout the Americas did indeed spring from ancient roots.[1]

[1] *America*, March 29, 1980.

Early in my tenure as pastor our organist was transferred from St. Louis. That led to the disbanding of the choir. The demise of the Visitation choir was a terrible sadness to the older parishioners. It seemed to be yet another coffin nail signifying imminent death for the parish. Fortunately, we were saved by the youth of the parish.

My pastoral assistant was young, vibrant and tireless Sister Maureen Minogue. One of her many "hats" was to coordinate a Saturday morning bible school. About half of the students in the bible school were members of Visitation. The others came for love, friendship and the assurance that on the last Saturday of every month they would be taken on a field trip. Part of the bible school schedule allowed time for the children to sing together.

When the students realized how dead the Sunday liturgy was without any music, they begged Maureen to help them start a youth choir. Maureen could play the three-chord guitar songs that were popular in the Vatican II church, and the youth were enthusiastic. Slowly, the youth choir grew, and then it became the center of controversy. As in most Catholic parishes after Vatican II, many members were disturbed by the silencing of the organ, the absence of the chant and the lack of the triumphal hymns. But, at Visitation the rift was deeper than that. It had a great deal to do with the generation gap and the growth of black awareness that had begun in the United States with the black-is-beautiful era. The young people heard their peers talk about singing in gospel choirs in their churches, and they felt called to that type of musical experience. The youngsters convinced Maureen that they ought to go to a neighboring Baptist church to hear the music.

The group members returned with two things emblazoned in their memories. The church they visited took up five collections, and the music was soulful and moving. A few of the youngsters brought records by James Cleveland and Andre Crouch, and in a few weeks some new songs made their way into the 11 o'clock liturgy. Some of the older members were not happy.

Traditionally, black Catholics have been middle class, and middle-class blacks have tried to disown the more fervid expressions of religion. It has been said that the social status of the black church can be determined by the ear: the higher the class, the less commotion and clapping. "We didn't become Catholic to hear all that Baptist music," some Visitation oldsters complained. "We don't need all that hand clappin' stuff in our church. This is a place to be quiet and reverent," others protested angrily.

And so the questions surfaced: What is religious? What is sacred? Why does anyone want to make distinctions between Catholics and black Catholics? The comments and controversy seemed unending.

As pastor, I found myself in a bind. On the one hand, the young people were exercising their initiative and giving their time and talent to the enrichment of the church's liturgy. On the other hand, older members of the church were questioning the Catholicity of their contribution. I, too, was confused; at one time I thought Luther's *A Mighty Fortress Is Our God* was more Catholic than the Negro spiritual *Go Down Moses*. And I certainly didn't know where James Cleveland and Mahalia Jackson fit in at all.

The older Catholics resented the mention of the word *black* in relation to Catholicism. They felt that the term was divisive. The young people felt they were being told to deny and be ashamed of their "blackground." That message was not being well received.

While these brushfires burned, the parish was trying to locate a new organist. We had two criteria: The musician should be competent, and he or she should be black. That was a laudable ideal, but it wasn't too realistic considering the small amount of money that the parish was able to pay. No black musicians responded to our ads. Fortunately, there were some good white musicians who responded, and we named Joe Scotti our organist. Joe was an excellent musician who had achieved his success in the face of crippling cerebral palsy. His warmth toward the young people was tempered by the interior toughness that he had had to develop as a handicapped person; he had pursued graduate studies in the face of constant ridicule and opposition and succeeded in earning a doctorate from the University of Cincinnati. Joe could relate to Visitation because he too had suffered from prejudice. As a handicapped person, he knew that racism was merely one of the forms of prejudice.

Now that we had an organist, we conducted a search for a choir director, again seeking a person both competent and black. This time we were successful. We located Linda Boyer, a black woman with a doctorate from Washington University. While the salaries paid to these excellent musicians were in no way lavish, they were enormous considering the limitations of the parish. However, this decision had to be made if we were to bring life to the worship.

To the delight of the parish and the envy of some neighboring churches, the Visitation Choir began to grow and develop once more into a proud choir. The struggle concerning "appropriate blackness" in the music still isn't solved. However, people persevere and periodically some strides are made.

Another dimension of liturgy that goes hand-in-hand with music is liturgical dance. Visitation has been blessed with the faithful presence of a multitalented woman named Erin Alexander. She has had years of voice and dance training and has been generous in sharing those gifts with the community. Her natural beauty and her talent are enhanced by her winning smile and charming personality. On those terms she is probably claimed as the sister or daughter of more parishioners than any other person.

Visitation is black Catholic, but these notions of inculturation also apply to other races and ethnic groups. If the church is to authentically touch the lives of the American Indians, the enormous Hispanic population, the Vietnamese and Haitians, then all the same rules must apply. We must view the people as variously gifted. In that light we must deal with them with loving care, knowing that every indigenous trait is a facet of the Creator's love.

9

FAILURE—CREATIVE STUMBLING

Seek the seeds of victory in every defeat.
—Ancient Chinese Proverb

The caliber of a man is found in his ability to meet disappointment successfully enriched rather than narrowed by it.
—Thomas R. Kelly
A Testament of Devotion

"They didn't mention this in the seminary," I thought as I approached my first ecumenical funeral. I had been invited to "say a few words over the deceased" so I had prepared a mimeographed bible service which included Psalm 23, "The Lord Is My Shepherd," to make it popular and adequately "non-Catholic." My entry into Gates Funeral Home with its spritely lobby fountain under a crystal chandelier was full of surprises.

There were 200 people spilling out of the chapel. A robed choir of 25 was standing by the electric organ to the right of the casket. As I entered the chapel, I received a pamphlet marked "Order of Service." Soon I discovered that I was the first of five preachers on the program. My head was spinning as I was ushered to the front and seated on a wooden folding chair far left of the pulpit, half-hidden by the standing floral sprays.

Happily I was the first minister on the program. This was

obviously going to be a long evening and I might have to leave early in view of the parish prayer group waiting for me to celebrate Mass with them. I led off with Psalm 23 and became an immediate hit as the crowd prayed along from memory. I preached from Paul, "Unless Jesus Christ is raised from the dead our faith is in vain and we above all are the most foolish of people." I warmed up as I heard a few enthusiastic "Amens" and even a "Preach on, Brother, tell us more." With the sweet smell of success surrounding my efforts and mingling with the fragrant bouquets, I explained that I would now defer to the next preacher on the program. He was gracious and even quoted "the Catholic priest" as he continued to build on the hope-resurrection theme.

After a few inspirational choir selections, I realized that 45 minutes had slipped by. I excused myself to return to the parish prayer group. I attempted to escape unnoticed down the side aisle, but a six-and-a-half footer tends to attract attention. Several people asked me if they could keep the mimeographed sheets, and one even asked me to write down my name and the name of my church. I smiled graciously and rekindled my youthful fantasies of Stan "the Man" Musial hounded by autograph seekers.

At last I escaped the press of the crowd, walking a bit taller as I left the air-conditioned comfort for the steamy pavement of a St. Louis summer. The sweet spirituals were drowned out by the traffic and people noises. Shouting children raced by boarded-up buildings chasing Frisbees. The racket of big wheels on the concrete created a grating noise only slightly less distracting than Concordes taking off. Teenagers bounced basketballs Globetrotter style and old-looking young men passed wine bottles in their brown bag disguises. I continued to gloat over my successful funeral ministry. I had touched hearts and gotten "Amens." However, I was still new to the night street scene and felt it in the pit of my stomach. My heart throbbed and the wetness in my palms was more than St. Louis humidity.

As I walked to my car I realized that my every step was being paced by the drone of a car whose engine strained in first gear. Out of the corner of my eye I saw a Buick from the dinosaur era of the '60s. It was a convertible bulging with young men sitting on the rear window ledge and standing on the floorboards. I wanted to run, but I was restrained by 16 eyes focused on my measured cadence. I tried futilely to be "cool" and ignore the rolling menace. That tiny voice of panic within was about to burst into a scream.

"Hey, Whitey!" The call split the heavy night air. I raised my eyes to attention.

In union the chorus rang out, "Honky, get your white ass out of our neighborhood." Some of the teen-agers on my side of the car punctuated their verbal demand with a hand gesture. The car sped away.

I covered the last block and reached my car with Olympic speed. Getting my key in the lock was complicated by my looking over my shoulder to see if the Buick was returning. Finally I was on my way back to Visitation.

Back at the parish, the waiting prayer group was getting worried. I related the incidents of the last hour, telling them how I had to develop a proper balance between popularity and intimidation. I had been "dressed down" from celebrity to honky all in a matter of minutes.

Strangely enough, my final evening in Ste. Genevieve Parish had prepared me for this situation, although at the time I had not been open to receiving the message. The parish threw a wonderful party for me and highlighted the contributions I had made to the community during the six years I had been associate pastor. Words of praise were lavished on me. People recounted my activities in the hospital, school and the larger community. The final speaker was my pastor, Monsignor Jim Holland.

Jim offered a few kind words of thanks, but then he closed with a cautious gospel reminder: "When you have done all you have been commanded to do, say, 'We are useless servants. We have done no more than our duty!' " (Lk 17:10).

The blunt truth of that statement which I would embrace later is a foundation piece regarding success and failure. It is tied in with cross-carrying, burden-sharing Christianity leading to new life.

Failure has its price in terms of draining fatigue and tedious depression. Failure has its blessings in terms of teaching us how to laugh and never to take ourselves too seriously. Failure is a good teacher. We all learn best from our mistakes. The challenge in the People Parish is to know how to enhance the positives and forgive and accept the negatives.

The Northside Food Co-op was the biggest early failure of my parish experience. It was a joint venture of our parish and the neighbors in St. Matthew's Parish. In less than one year, the co-op lost several thousand dollars and had numerous volunteers on the verge of burnout. When the effort was finally disbanded and money raised to pay the bad debts, it was clear that the main shortcoming of the project was the lack of grassroots direction. The founding of the food co-op had been due largely to my collaborative efforts with Father Bill Hutchinson, founder of the Northside Community Center. While many other projects of Northside are successful, the food co-op required something different—large numbers of volunteers. Adequate volunteers simply were not available for the demanding long hours on Thursdays that would make the venture succeed. The notion that volunteers would somehow surface had been wishful thinking.

Another project doomed to frustration and finally to failure was the opening of the Visitation Youth Center for evening and weekend study and recreation. Lloyd White was a person of good looks, considerable education, poise, vision and athletic prowess. When he came to the parish to pursue the idea of a community center in the school gym, I was intrigued. Lloyd's graduate education with some background in guidance and counseling was a gift. These are important skills in any youth minister, but in the inner-city they are invaluable. I reacted quickly and hired Lloyd in violation of one of my most cherished principles. I failed to talk with the parish council and with those people who would be most clearly touched by Lloyd's presence. In this case, I should have spoken with some of the parish and neighborhood youth who knew better than I what their hopes and aspirations for a youth minister were. I jumped the gun and hired Lloyd without consultation. When he resigned somewhat later the Visitation School building was closed and did not find new life until the conception and opening of the Visitation Child Development Center.

There were other failures. I have already mentioned some of them—the closing of the parish school, the management difficulties at the credit union, and my failure to organize a finance committee. There is no infallible ratio concerning hard work and success. I am certain that some of the people involved in the "failures" invested more time and energy than did some of the people involved in the "successes." That is not to say they were ineffective or misguided. Failure is a part of the condition of human nature. Rising up from failure is as Christian a concern as repentance from sin and resurrection from the dead.

Lack of significant planning and grassroots community support seem to be common to the failures we suffered. There is a fine line that must be walked between sufficient planning and research on one hand and an atmosphere that paralyzes people and stifles all spontaneity on the other. One of the general principles I used in regard to starting new projects was this: Don't build hope in hopeless people just so their hopes can be dashed again by failure. I was concerned that new projects have some hope of staying power. The '60s spawned too many projects that failed as soon as government funds dried up. I think it is cruel to paint a picture of hope that is likely to self-destruct. Yet caution should be balanced with the saying of Chardin, "What paralyzes life is not to dream and not to dare." A life without failures would be a life closed to dreaming and daring, and hence no life at all.

Another principle concerning growth is both biblical and agricultural. It is that some people plant and water, and other people reap the harvest. All structural change is tedious. Tending and nurturing of projects is an important aspect of living. In families, young people need a lot of encouragement and challenging before they show clear signs of character development and mature adulthood. The same thing can be said for projects that involve large numbers of people and social change. The planting and watering is often an unheralded and thankless job.

The person who fails well can never be defeated. Once a person rises up from failure, from hopelessness, chaos and utter disaster, that person is unbeatable. That person knows the freedom of living life with gusto and relatively free from fear.

Life invites us to discover the hope assured by the fact that our God does not know failure. Apparent failure is the grain of wheat dying or the brother and sister laying down their lives for a friend. At worst, failure is creative stumbling; at best, it is being born to eternal life.

> My brothers [and sisters], consider it a great joy when trials of many kinds come upon you, for you well know that the testing of your faith produces perseverance and perseverance must complete its work so that you will become fully developed, complete, not deficient in any way (Jas 1:2-4, *New Jerusalem Bible*).

10

IS THERE LIFE AFTER FATHER GERRY?

If you can't walk the walk, don't talk the talk.

—Anonymous

Many receive advice, only the wise profit by it.

—Publilius Syrus

Several years into my first assignment in Ste. Genevieve I was working late at my desk. During a moment of distraction I noticed the lights at the office of the Ste. Genevieve Building Stone Company directly across the street. I was curious about their late hours, and I was questioning my own sanity in working past 10:00 p.m. I walked across the street and found Bob Uding pondering a bid for a construction job. With a little coaxing he decided it was time to quit and pour a drink. We talked about the old days when his dad started the business as a limestone quarry.

In telling the story of the growth of the business, he mentioned hiring the first non-family employees and the unionizing of the company. He remembered that it was a trauma for his dad when the first employee left the company. Until that time he had viewed them all as closely as he did his three sons.

One afternoon a worker presented himself in a rather arrogant fashion making some demands and threatening to quit if they weren't met. Country-strong John Uding asked the man to do him a favor. He pointed to the water bucket with the ladle hooked over the side. "Bend over there and put your fist into the pail of water," he directed. The man obliged. "Now take it out," he requested. The man did. "You see how big a dent you left in that water when you pulled your hand out? That's just how big a dent you're going to leave in this company when you quit here." John turned and walked away. The man knew he had just become a former employee.

Maybe the story is a little calloused; however, the point is clear. Any project or organization of substance is not dependent on one person. The Union stayed together after Lincoln was assassinated. The Second Vatican Council continued after Pope John XXIII died. And Notre Dame played a lot of winning football after the plane carrying Knute Rockne crashed. None of us leaves a dent when we pull out. There is life after all of us.

I believe that a pastor shouldn't stay in a parish for over 10 years. Otherwise he is liable to get possessive and start to refer to my church, my school, my rectory and my playground. Furthermore, he might not be open to new ideas and directions for the parish. I always knew I would leave Visitation in 1983 at the time of my 10th anniversary. To prepare for that, I decided to do something in 1982 at the time of my 40th birthday.

As my birthday approached in January, I decided to do a half-life inventory. I knew that by actuarial scales I had lived half my life. In the spirit of the half-time shows on television sports, I thought it was time to recap and plan new strategies. What had I done in the first half? What should I do in the last half? I sent letters asking people—family, friends and critics—for a very specific birthday present.

> In the middle of January I will celebrate my 40th birthday. I have been thinking about several things in relation to this event. The most important thought has been about the direction of my life during the next 40 years, or whatever time might remain to me.
>
> I have never sought (and seldom received) responses from the people around me as to how they perceive me.

> Therefore, I would like to ask you and a number of other persons to do two things for me in preparation for this event. Would you please jot down a couple of weaknesses which I should address as I prepare for the second half of my life? (Sort of a see-ourselves-as-others-see-us input.)
>
> If I can receive candid feedback from friends, fellow workers, business associates and relatives, I can face the rest of my life and its tasks more intelligently and productively.
>
> I am very serious in my request, and I'd be very grateful if you would take the time to help me with this self-examination.
>
> I have enclosed a self-addressed, stamped envelope. Thank you for your time and your help.

I sent letters to 25 people; 18 people took the time to respond. Even Brother Gene Garcia, S.J., who writes letters so seldom that he would never notice a year-long postal strike, responded. When I received a letter from Gene, I knew it was correspondence from a man of few written words. They deserved attentive reading.

In a very pointed way Gene told me it was time to act according to the words I had always spoken. I had talked much about empowering people and recognizing their dignity. If I really believed that, it was time to move on and hand the parish and the community projects over to the people.

The responses to those letters confirmed my belief that 10 years as pastor were enough. The details of leaving Visitation were still very foggy. I anticipated that the decision would be lonely; it would call for some creative, reform-minded thinking within the church.

The problem was not just a problem of my leaving and finding a new type of assignment. The larger, more significant concern was the selection of a new pastor. The choosing of a new pastor in the Archdiocese of St. Louis in 1982 involved no parochial participation. A priest received a letter assigning him to become pastor of a new parish, and off he went. There was little consultation on the decision. There was no personnel director. Certainly, we would have to plan carefully in order to help the system to work as efficiently as possible.

Our first step was to copy the procedures of Protestant churches. We borrowed several questionnaires, outlining the qualities, experience and vision that the parishioners desired in a new pastor. We gleaned the best questions and were careful to cross out references to women pastors. After several discussions at the parish council, a final form was chosen. The questionnaires were printed and prepared for mailing to the parishioners. It was unclear to us how we would utilize the results of this process, but we trusted that the information would be beneficial.

On the very morning the questionnaires were to be mailed, I sat at my desk and glanced at the form one last time. This time I thought about the type of information that the process was likely to reveal. I feared that everyone would be looking for a person so gifted and experienced that only Jesus would be a suitable candidate. And even if a less than divine person would fill the bill, where would we find him? There was no corresponding list of priestly gifts, talents and desires. When the janitor came to mail the letters I stopped him. "Creed, don't take this. I don't think we're going to use this mailing after all."

I felt like a fool as I began to phone the officers of the parish council. I contacted each one and began my long explanation. "I'm sitting here and thinking that this questionnaire won't help us in the selection of a new pastor. It seems to me that it would only work if there were some corresponding information bank that listed the qualities and talents of the diocesan priests. Without that, we are wasting the time that the parishioners will use in answering the questions. Further, we are wasting time tallying their responses. We'll have to sit down again and decide on a new more workable pastoral selection plan."

"If you just decided to stay here, we wouldn't have to do all this work and everyone would be happy," pleaded Gwen, my secretary.

I was back to the drawing boards and we began anew

with meetings to determine how to pick a pastor. The whole procedure uncovered many fears in the minds of the parishioners.

One fear was that this was a new and radical thing to do. We were liable to get in trouble with the archbishop. I assured them that John May had shown our parish great love. He had visited us several times and complimented the work we had undertaken. I agreed with them that our approach was radical, but it was no more radical that starting an integrated school in 1946.

Second, the people feared that no priest would want to come to the parish. "I think you sell yourselves too short, and I think you are harsh in your evaluation of St. Louis priests," I protested. "I'm sure that many priests are interested in this church. I promise you I can find some priests who would be proud to consider being pastor here. The parish has a fine reputation."

Last, the people were convinced we would get in trouble. That vague fear meant we might rattle the system so badly that the decision-makers would use this as an excuse to close the parish. Everyone knew there were too many parishes in the inner city.

There wasn't a clear-cut answer to that fear. We would have to trust more in the good will of the archbishop. We would have to believe that the efforts, successes and history of black Catholicism at Visitation could not be ignored. And we would have to resist the temptation to view ourselves as powerless. We were the home of the SLACO organization, a viable and articulate community group. Just as SLACO had confronted oppression and political power when it was exercised in an abusive fashion, so we could confront church systems if it became necessary.

Those fears cast aside, it was time to get back to planning. My job was to find 12 priests who would come to meet and talk with the people. They would experience the gifts of the Visitation community and then decide if they would like to be the pastor. They would not come to be interviewed. They would *never* be interrogated. They would be welcomed.

People said, "Don't invite anyone who is a pastor. A pastor

anywhere else would consider it a demotion to come to Visitation." Others said, "Don't invite anyone who is working in another inner-city parish. If he is doing a good job there, let's not rob Peter to pay Paul. Let's not try to build our success by undermining the work of a neighboring church." With those guidelines I went to work calling friends and acquaintances who had good reputations as holy, hard-working priests.

The parish council had a new project to replace the tabulating of the discarded survey. They were to oversee the writing of a booklet on the parish organizations and activities. Each of the projects would be described in less than two pages. The final part of each narrative would be the listing of names, addresses and phone numbers of people currently involved in the project. From the most technical corporations like the Credit Union to the most catholic, like the Liturgy Committee, to the most social like the Jetsetters, to the most in-house like the Altar society, all were to be included. The descriptions were to be honest and humble enough to admit the faults and deficiencies; for example, the Youth Group was more a dream than a reality, but there were a few people plugging along. The idea was to present an honest description of the works and commitments of the parish. The genius was in the lists. These would inform the new pastor that real people embodied these projects. Their names and phone numbers would be further assurance that they were available to help. The unspoken message was: "We're by your side to help you. Count on us. Dial the phone when you need us."

The book was completed, corrected, typed and mimeographed. The priests were contacted, and 10 agreed to attend a Saturday morning meeting. The people were still leery about the wisdom of the whole approach. "Father Gerry always comes up with these 'off the wall' ideas. Why don't we just let the bishop appoint a new pastor and let well enough alone? We'll do all this work and no one will pay any attention."

In the face of that lingering worry, I received an inspiration. I have one classmate, Tom Michel, who works in the Vatican. Tom has a great love for Visitation Parish because his grandfather was one of the Irish immigrants who hastened the formation of the parish in 1882.

I wrote to Tom and told him of our pastoral selection process. I told him of the fears of people that this was arrogant and possibly fruitless. I told him we had never envisioned this as a foolproof scheme or a way to manipulate the archbishop. The archbishop knew we would accept and welcome a new pastor who had never been a part of the process.

I wrote, "Tom, in view of the parish nervousness please get us the largest, most attractive papal blessing that is available in Rome. Have it worded in a way that highlights the love and esteem Pope John Paul II has for the people of Visitation Parish Family. In short, the blessing ought to indicate that if Pope John Paul II could be here, he *would* be here."

It was a joyful day when the mailman brought the cardboard tube from Rome. Tom had surpassed my most enthusiastic expectations with the design and wording of the blessing. I called Roy and Carrie Torian, faithful members with impeccable taste in picture framing. "Would you frame the blessing and participate in the prayer service at the meeting? The papal blessing will be hung next to the Easter Candle and behind the statue of the Black Madonna of Montserrat." Ron and Carrie were honored and delighted to help.

The parish grapevine is more effective than the bulletin for carrying news. Tenseness and excitement grew as the pastoral selection Saturday approached. All the details seemed to be in order and 50 people had signed up to attend.

As I leaned back in the chair that I was about to relinquish to a new pastor, I thought about Saturday and the meeting. I worried about the weather and the attendance. About one thing I was certain. Every detail in planning this meeting had been communicated to the archbishop. I was confident that the diocese knew exactly what we were going to do. I was very proud of that.

Everything about the Saturday meeting was more successful than I could have ever imagined. The weather was fine, the attendance was good and the first people to arrive were the priests who came from rural parishes and spent over an hour on the road. Spirits were high, and there was an air of expectancy as we gathered. It was the birth of a new dimension of church. Everyone knew that this type of meeting would be a first in their lives as Catholics. Some knew of pastoral selections from their Protestant background. Others knew the early church had elected bishops. But none had ever been in this historic Catholic setting. Electricity filled the gym.

After donuts and coffee, the meeting was begun with a half-hour of prayer. There was gratitude to God for the hard work and courage that had brought us to the day in the same historic school where black and white children had broken the color barrier almost 40 years earlier. There was gratitude for the priests, religious and people who gathered at this oasis of hope. Finally, there was joy and celebration when the papal blessing was enthroned and Carrie Torian told of her pride in having this parchment in her home during the time of its framing. It said, "Pope John Paul II sends his warmest fraternal greeting and apostolic benediction on the Visitation Parish Family." Spirituals were sung and the Easter Candle was lit.

The meeting progressed in a well-rehearsed and ordered fashion. Each of the people who wrote a section on a parish organization or activity had three minutes to synopsize their project. The assembly followed along with the booklet. If anything important had been overlooked, people mentioned that information and a note was made for future revisions. In an hour that portion of the meeting was completed. There was a general sense of enthusiasm regarding the many parish endeavors. Many people who were active in one aspect of parish life had their eyes opened to other areas.

After a brief break the meeting moved to the next phase. It was a time of planning for the future. The idea was to give the new pastor a sense of current parish commitments and also a taste of where the parish would like to move in the future. The booklet categorized past and ongoing endeavors; the brainstorming would get us into the future mode. The people were divided into small groups and each of these had a group leader and a secretary. Each of the groups was asked to share ideas regarding the future of Visitation. These could be as diverse as starting a Girl Scout troop to painting yellow lines on the parking lot. No idea would be immediately rejected; neither would any idea receive immediate approbation.

After half an hour, the brainstorming was concluded and

each leader came to the front of the auditorium and presented the group's ideas. Notes written on a large piece of newsprint were taped to the wall in plain view of everyone. When all the groups had been heard, ballots were distributed and each person was invited to vote for his or her two top choices. The ballots were counted, and the six most popular ideas were indicated to the gathered assembly. These would be explained in the parish bulletin over the course of the next six weeks. Then the entire parish would have a chance to vote for the two best ideas. These would become the future directives for the new pastor.

The significance of this approach is to make the work of the new pastor as easy as possible. He can begin with confidence, knowing that many of the existing organizations and activities have a life of their own. Certainly, if he chooses to be involved, he is welcome. If he does not, that is his choice.

It also sidesteps a danger new pastors frequently face, that is, people expect them to adopt their particular pet project. In fact, some of the first people to get to the new pastor are the very people who do nothing; they are only good at telling the priest what he should do. Our method of future planning avoids that pitfall. The pastor can say he has a mandate to work in two specified areas, and that other ideas will have to be put on hold.

At 12:45 the meeting was about to adjourn. The only task remaining was to introduce the priests who had come to be with us. For several hours they had been listeners. Now they would have the chance to say something about themselves and their impressions of Visitation. I introduced them with some brief background information. Some of the priests had spent time in other inner-city parishes, and several had been with the St. Louis missionary effort in Bolivia or Chile. One of the candidates, Bill Kester, had been a high school teacher living in residence at Visitation nine years earlier.

When he was introduced, Bill responded, "I always remember my time at Visitation with great fondness. When I left here you gave me a beautiful stole and whenever I wear it I remember friends and happy days here. That's been a long time ago now, and I've seen this parish grow in many ways. The best way for me to sum up this meeting is to say this. After the first hour of the meeting, I said to myself: 'These people are proud.' After the second hour of the meeting, I said, 'These people are darn proud.' Now that we've come to this point, I'm happy to say aloud, you people have something here to be very proud of." The applause was deafening as Bill sat down.

In the next six weeks, articles were printed in the parish bulletin about possible future goals. After each had been explained and highlighted, a vote was taken. The two areas the people selected for future development were youth ministry and improved music for the liturgy. At the same time five priests expressed an openness to being named the pastor of Visitation.

A complete report of the meeting was forwarded to the archbishop and the Committee for the Life and Ministry of Priests. As pastoral candidates expressed their interest in the position, we forwarded their names to the diocese. We always accompanied that information with a sentence in the letter that stated our willingness to accept whoever might be assigned to the parish.

Several weeks later I received a phone call from Charlie Burgoon, the president of the personnel board. He said, "I guess I ought to come over and visit and talk with you about a new pastor for Visitation Parish."

I was shocked and delighted by the phone call. I had never heard of that happening in any other parish in St. Louis. I invited him over for lunch and a visit around the parish. I barely had the phone back in its cradle when I began to think about parishioners who might be able to take some time to join us for lunch. Everyone I called was excited about Charlie's interest.

After the lunch and before the more formal conversation, we played a tape recording of the talk Archbishop John May had give at the 100th anniversary of Visitation Parish just five months earlier. In his talk he recognized the great manifestation of church that was represented not only in liturgy, but in the efforts of the Visitation Community Credit Union, SLACO, the Visitation Child Development Center and other community projects. Charlie listened to the tape and realized that Visitation was a prayer community with a firm commitment to an outer life of service. After a conversation around the dining-room table, several of the parishioners had to return to work. Then Charlie and I took a walk over to the child development center. Finally we retired to my room for a conversation regarding the merits of the priests who had applied for the position. He spent over three hours at Visitation.

By the time of Charlie's visit, I had a new job. I had been offered the position of Director of Diocesan Seminarians at Moreau Seminary at the University of Notre Dame. When the invitation came, it was rather vague. I showed it to Archbishop May and asked him if I could pursue it. He said he would be open to that, but I should take the time to go to Notre Dame and work out the details more clearly. I was happy to do that, and the three-day meeting at Moreau Seminary was reassuring. We negotiated on a job description and a salary. They offered me $1,000 more than I asked for; I was happy to oblige.

In May the new assignments came out, and a pastor was appointed. Robert Zinser, one of the Saturday morning candidates, had eight years previous experience in inner-city ministry. When he arrived on the scene, I didn't have to drive him through the neighborhood because he knew it already. He called me the evening the mail came to tell me of his appointment. We had known each other for years and had a wonderful love-hate relationship. In his deep, gravelly voice he said, "Well, Kleba, I'm coming to Visitation. When are you getting out of there so I can move in?"

I was delighted. I wanted to hug him over the phone. I could leave happy. "It is finished!"

My final bit of Visitation good news came in the form of a postscript handwritten by Archbishop May on the bottom of my letter of appointment to Notre Dame. It read, "Stop by and have lunch with me before you leave." I called to make an appointment and enjoyed the lunch at the Archbishop's residence. After lunch he asked me if I had time to visit, and we retired to the living room of this elegant turn-of-the-century mansion.

"How did you proceed with the pastoral selection program at Visitation?" he asked.

At first I was tempted to be very brief because I had sent

him packets of information in the mail. Then I thought about how slow I was to read similar collections received in manila envelopes. Now I felt he was saying, "Tell me how you pulled that off so successfully." I told the story in some detail. He listened very attentively and nodded and smiled in all the right places. I was very pleased.

Finally, he had to return to his office. He walked with me to my car, and we talked about the possibility of his coming to see a Notre Dame football game. As we reached the car, we shook hands with a double clasp and he said, "Enjoy yourself at Notre Dame and do well there. Remember, we are very proud of you."

11

VISITATION REVISITED— ALIVE AND GROWING

The final test of a leader is that he leaves behind him in other men the conviction and the will to carry on.

—Walter Lippmann
Roosevelt Has Gone

The refuge from pessimism is the good men and women existing at any time in the world—they keep faith and happiness alive.

—Charles E. Norton
(1827-1908)

Since Visitation is a living community, no one would expect it to be exactly the same as when I left it in June of 1983. Visitation has continued to grow and develop and has begun to take on some of the personality of the new pastor, Father Bob Zinser. In his 1984 Easter letter he stated:

> This is my first Easter at Visitation and some reflections seem in order. . . . Even though Holy Week can be a little tiring for all of us, I personally find myself renewed and freshened by the faith of the people of Visitation whom I have had the time to get to know a little

> better. And you have opened your hearts to me and even though less than a year is still not enough time, I look forward to ever-deepening bonds between all of us—bonds that give new life, new insights, new growth. I, for one, know that Jesus is truly risen and that he will give me new life at the resurrection. And I know it not because of a theology book but because I have seen him doing it already through you. I hope that all the people of Visitation are saying the same thing on this Easter Day, 1984.

In less than one year Father Bob was able to experience the lived love of Jesus and the hope of the resurrection incarnate in the Visitation Parish Family.

In contrast to the reaching-out approach of my pastorate, the parish under Father Bob has taken a new direction. While the variety of social ministries has continued and thrived, the bulk of pastoral direction has been concentrated on close-to-home endeavors. This is the dynamic of life. There are times to reach out and stretch oneself; there are times to probe deep within. The two are mutually supportive and authentic. One does not sacrifice the other, but one enhances the other. It is like breathing in and breathing out.

In my observations of the parish from 350 miles away, I think the best new endeavor has been the restructuring of the parish council. I never did much work along that line. I knew from the beginning that it was lacking, but it never made my own list of priorities. Bob tackled it almost immediately, knowing that it could be an important determinant of the quality of parish life. By November 11, 1984, there was a parish assembly. Judging from the brochure prepared for the occasion, things were running much more smoothly.

Improving liturgical music was one of the directives the parish gave the new pastor at the Pastoral Selection Day. That task became more formidable when the excellent choir director, Eugene Thomas, had to resign because of a promotion at work. That was unexpected, but it was not the type of obstacle that caused people to throw in the towel. Even as the choir was looking for a new director, the parish sponsored a workshop on gospel music. The day was presented by Robert J. Ray of the

St. Louis Conservatory for the Arts and was open to neighborhood parishes and guests.

The second mandate was for a better youth ministry. It is my impression from visiting the parish that there are more youngsters and young adults active in worship and other projects. The number of teen events seems to have increased. The parish has hired a youth minister in cooperation with neighboring Holy Rosary Parish. This joint effort might be quite successful since there are so few Catholic youth and young people are so gregarious.

A totally new involvement for Visitation is participation in and support of the Lwanga Center. Lwanga is a retreat and lay ministry training center for the black community that is the cooperative effort of about 10 neighboring parishes. While there are other adult education programs for the diocese as a whole, Lwanga has the advantage of being located in the black community and governed by a local board. It offers an alternative structure of religious leader formation more responsive to black culture and to the needs of the sponsors. It is located in the heart of the community. "Crossroads," a day of faith sharing and community building, is one of the Lwanga programs.

Another form of education and community building is the follow-up to the RENEW program. The parish topic of Lent 1985 was the black bishops' pastoral, "What We Have Seen and Heard."

Another new project conceived in the parish is called "Catalyst." The October 30, 1983, bulletin says:

> A Catalyst is a point of contact where something happens that otherwise would not. Our Catalyst Program is the point of contact where Jesus' love meets our sick and confined parishioners. If we can help you by putting you in contact with a brother or sister you could call or drive somewhere, call Bernice Page at the rectory.

"Catalyst" invites people, even people who are normally thought to need help, to serve others to the best of their ability.

Since I left Visitation, Bishop Healy school has grown. St. Adalbert Parish School has joined the consolidated school.

Bishop Healy has also opened a computer center and received accreditation.

Stacy Murray continues to be as reliable as Old Faithful in his work for the poor through the St. Vincent de Paul Society. Operation Food Search has located huge quantities of food from various processors and wholesalers. Stacy writes, "We have been very busy. Operation Search has been calling us every week and sometimes twice a week to pick up food. They are getting food in 40-foot trailers." Since 5 million more people have fallen below the poverty guidelines since 1980, that type of help is invaluable.

The Visitation Child Development Center continues to function, but the enrollment has decreased. One reason is the shortage of government funding for day-care centers. Despite that, Visitation continues to offer scholarships.

The area of the People Parish that is the clearest example of growth and success is the Visitation Community Credit Union. The current financial sheet shows $1.5 million in assets and only nine delinquent loans. The credit union offers VISA cards and checking accounts.

SLACO continues its efforts at community organizing. Several new areas have been added to the organization. Growth in community organizations can best be measured by perceived strength and noteworthy achievements. Recently, SLACO has been instrumental in passing a city law and a state law.

The St. Louis Resident Jobs Policy should create job openings for minorities in the most depressed areas of St. Louis. The intent is clear and simple. When the city hires contractors to work, SLACO wants to see that many of the salaries are paid to city residents. They then pay city taxes and improve the standard of living in St. Louis. It's not selfish; it is enlightened self-interest.

The state law concerns housing occupancy. In order to end the exploits of slum landlords, the new statute demands that when a person purchases a tax-delinquent house at a sheriff's sale, that house must be brought up to city code before it can be sold to a new owner. Previously these homes were resold at a profit to poor, unsuspecting people. When they missed their first monthly payment, they were evicted and the sale process was done once more. This became increasingly lucrative as the numbers of homeless increased in our society.

Both of these efforts on the part of SLACO required cooperation and outreach far beyond the black community.

The housing efforts that during my time at Visitation had been mainly rehabilitation and homesteading entered a whole new field. After years of dreaming and planning, new single-family units are being built on vacant lots. The first project will produce 28 affordable, energy-efficient homes in the city.

Happily, the largest projects begun at the People Parish—the credit union, the child development center and SLACO are alive and vigorous. Father Bob serves on the child center board; the other projects flourish without official participation on his part. That is the way they were designed. That allows Bob freedom to do the things that best suit his talents and current parish needs.

Finally, Charlean Armstead of Visitation has become involved in an archdiocesan program that could have profound and far-reaching implications for the entire church. She is a member of the Task Force on Women, the local archdiocesan effort to prepare for the future pastoral letter. It is a touchy job because there are so many strong feelings about feminism in the church. The whole question is complicated because of an inclination in the church hierarchy to treat women as the problem rather than seeing that sexism in the church is a major human-rights issue.

It was Charlean who closed a letter to me with a poem by an unknown author. It says a lot about the dynamics of the People Parish:

> When faced with a mountain
> I will not quit!
> I will keep on striving until I
> Climb over, find a pass through,
> Tunnel underneath—or simply
> Stay and turn the mountain
> Into a gold mine, with God's help!